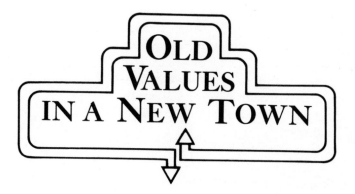

OLD
VALUES
IN A NEW TOWN

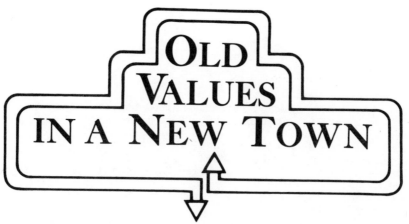

The Politics of Race and Class in Columbia, Maryland

Lynne C. Burkhart

Foreword by Peter H. Rossi

PRAEGER

PRAEGER SPECIAL STUDIES • PRAEGER SCIENTIFIC

Library of Congress Cataloging in Publication Data

Burkhart, Lynne C
    Old values in a new town.

    Bibliography: p.
    Includes index.
    1. New towns--Social aspects--United States--
Case studies. 2. Columbia, Md.--Race relations--
Case studies. 3. Social classes--Maryland--
Columbia--Case studies. 4. Quality of life--
Maryland--Columbia--Case studies. 5. Social con-
flict--Case studies. 6. Columbia, Md.--Social
conditions. I. Title.
HT164.U6B87   307.7'6'0973   80-26556
ISBN 0-03-058306-3

Published in 1981 by Praeger Publishers
CBS Educational and Professional Publishing
A Division of CBS, Inc.
521 Fifth Avenue, New York, New York 10175 U.S.A.

123456789 145 987654321

Printed in the United States of America

FOREWORD

Since the end of World War II, America's urban problems appeared to grow faster than noxious weeds and to be increasingly more difficult to remedy. Central cities became more unattractive to middle-class populations, while the expanding suburbs promised to provide an endless supply for tomorrow's slums. Nor were central cities pleasant places for the working classes and the new immigrant streams. The metropolitan areas showed every promise of becoming black at the core and white in the periphery, with a correspondingly firm cleavage in politics between the interests of the two.

In the context of those decades of despair, a few bright spots appeared. Among the brightest were the new towns that showed promise of building communities free of the baggage of the past, towns that could accomodate reasonably well-planned physical environments with the potential for class and racial harmony in heterogeneous communities. The archetypal new town was Columbia, Maryland. A farsighted, socially conscious, and economically sound developer, James W. Rouse, assembled a building site and brought together skillful planners, social scientists, and good financing to build a city for 100,000 people halfway between Baltimore, Maryland and Washington, D. C.

Many hopes went into Columbia. There was the hope of providing a well-planned community physical environment, with plentiful open space and well-placed amenities. There was the hope that the villages and neighborhoods of Columbia would form the building blocks of a community consciousness ordinarily lost in suburban sprawl, which would contribute to improving the quality of life for all residents. In many respects most important, and surely most controversial, was the hope of insuring a reasonable mix of income levels and races, a mix that did not seem to occur in older places or in conventional suburban developments.

The goal of interracial and interclass harmony and cooperation is firmly ensconced in the postwar egalitarian ideology of our liberal, well-educated population. If, instead of experiencing each other as stereotypes who brush past one another in public places, people could get together in the same community and experience each other as human beings, the ideological goal of substantive equality could be achieved.

Columbia has achieved that goal, at least on the surface. Blacks constitute about 20 percent of the current Columbia population. The housing types are heterogeneous in price so that there is some mixing of income levels, and federally subsidized units can be found in close proximity to housing of substantial cost. But, more important, neither race nor class has surfaced as an issue in the developing polity of Columbia. A superficial acquaintance with Columbia would bear these statements out.

A more penetrating look at the new town, however, would unearth a more complicated structure, as this book relates. Dr. Lynne Burkhart lived in Columbia for several years, participated in its life at many levels, and observed with the sensitive mind of a social anthropologist. Her analysis of the micropolitics of Columbia shows that race and class are still central issues in policy controversies in that town, while clothed in a number of semantic disguises. In the political rhetoric of Columbia, the mention of black and white, rich and poor, is taboo; for those who closely attend to the local glossary, however, the rhetoric can be translated into familiar terms.

It would be easy to regard Dr. Burkhart's report as documenting the intransigency of race and class as basic cleavages in our society. Yet such an interpretation would not be justified. The submersion of such issues below the surface can also be interpreted as meaning that Columbia residents are successfully working out issues, particularly those of race, in ways that both shed light on some of the puzzling areas of impasse of the past and foreshadow new modes of interracial and interclass accommodation.

The new town movement in the United States now appears to be either dead or dormant. Inflation, federal policy changes, and the spoiling of the housing market have meant that financing for new towns will be unavailable in the foreseeable future. It may be that a few years hence, federal policy will again favor new towns. A strong market for new construction may reappear, and builders, lenders, and planners may feel optimistic about investing in land, planning a community, and building the homes and amenities involved. For the moment, however, the new town movement has come to a halt. Columbia may be the best example of successful new town building ever.

Whatever the future of the new town movement, the urbanist can profit from Dr. Burkhart's portrait of the politics of race and class in Columbia. If we are to progress in our understanding of community and society, we must learn from the successes and failures of the past.

Peter H. Rossi

ACKNOWLEDGMENTS

Case studies usually require a continual presence and a ruthless probing, and in the process impose on the intellectual and personal generosity of many who are integral to the social processes one observes. This study is no exception. Staff at the Columbia Association and the Columbia Interfaith Housing Corporation, in particular Roger Ralph and Joseph M. Marshall, offered access to much needed materials and comfortable work space. I am grateful to them, and to the countless others who also displayed unflagging interest in my work and offered their experiences, thoughts, and friendship during the 18 months of data gathering in Columbia, Maryland.

The field work was funded by the National Institute for Mental Health (1 R01 MH 25598), and I am grateful for interest and support from the Center for Metropolitan Problems. I am particularly indebted to Elliot Liebow, whose sensitive analysis of street corner life and whose support for my ideas about Columbia led to this study.

The earlier manuscript from which this book is drawn owes much to my eminent teacher and thoughtful friend, Peter H. Rossi. His respect for my anthropological frame of analysis and his prompt and voluminous response, both enthusiastic and critical, to innumerable memos and drafts during every phase of the research and writing are among my debts to him. That all of his enthusiasms have been absorbed and some of his criticisms overlooked means, of course, that he is not responsible for any shortcomings of the analysis.

I am grateful to Geoffrey L. Burkhart for the contributions of his uniquely sensitive eyes and ears during the research and his careful editings of several early drafts.

My largest and happiest debt is to Jud, Denni, and Carol for their unmeasured enthusiasm and support. I dedicate this study to them, and to their continued liberation from filial and sex roles.

CONTENTS

INTRODUCTION

In the spring of 1971, my husband, three children, and I moved from a racially integrated neighborhood in Washington, D.C. to Columbia, Maryland, the new town located between Washington and Baltimore, Maryland. Our decision to move to a planned community was not an easy one, for the pros and cons of new town living were discussed a great deal in Washington and Baltimore in those days. On the one hand, the immensely successful public relations effort of the developer was translated into an image of a rewarding, quasi-urban life, successfully eliminating the evils associated with urban areas in the preceding decades and with the social and physical homogeneity of American suburban life. People talked about the unusual amounts of open space and the high quality of community services and recreational facilities. They stressed the absence of crime, heavy traffic, and large, ugly advertising signs and overhead wiring.

There were, on the other hand, many critics. They warned of the sterility of a planned community and of the commitment to community activities that was said to be required of all residents. Their comments suggested that it was just too much trouble, and probably more than a little boring, to live in Columbia.

There was one point that was agreed upon in all the talk: the developer had made a genuine effort to build a community that did not exclude anyone by standards of race or class, to actively recruit black residents by using carefully designed marketing techniques, and to support, with a land subsidy for lower income housing, the concept of an economically mixed community. It was this remarkable effort, and the measure of success it had achieved, that was Columbia's attraction for us and for a large number of others who moved there in the early years.

My social scientist friends predicted that I would lose my identity, and certainly my free time, in the pressure for citizen participation. They were wrong. I lived in Columbia for two years, before beginning to study it, without voting in local elections, untouched by committees, and continuing most of my social contacts in Washington, where I had lived for many years, and in Baltimore among graduate student colleagues.

At the same time, however, I felt a strong attachment to the community, the source of which seemed mysterious given my general lack of involvement in active community life. I now think this was a reaction to being part, however peripheral, of a goal-oriented, purposive community. Especially in the early days, the most important goal was a better life for many different kinds of people, particularly for blacks and for those with lower incomes. Indeed, James Rouse, the mortgage banker and developer of Columbia, was considered courageous to plan this kind of racial and class mixing in the mid-1960s, and it is not surprising that I was caught up in the community feeling that was forged around it.

It seemed that living in a "truly integrated" community was important to most people's sense of belonging. Residents talked publicly and privately about the good feeling between blacks and whites in public places. Several years later I still feel that the combination of mutual respect, assertiveness, and friendliness that characterizes casual contacts between blacks and whites in Columbia is unusual enough that it ought never to be minimized as a powerful political and social phenomenon. This racial openness is at once Columbia's most notable success, a catalyst for community spirit, a potential for an important social change in the lives of both black and white residents, and an area where failure would be devastating—to the developer, to property owners, and perhaps most important, to believers in the traditional model of integration, of whom there are still many.

We lived in Columbia for four years: two before this study began and two during which I was a researcher and then a writer. Continued private acknowledgment of "a race problem among teens" kept reminding me of impressions I had formed during the first few months we lived there. The high school, for example, had just opened and was "already socially segregated by race." Occasional incidents of violence following the use of racial epithets of both black and white students were reported.

Yet I sensed a different dynamic than I had experienced in either inner-city schools where blacks had been in a large majority, or in urban and suburban schools where racial violence followed an influx of black students after court-ordered busing. While social separation between black and white youth in Columbia's high school was pervasive, competition seemed for the most part good natured, broken only occasionally by an unusual incident.

Furthermore, because it was the first high school within the boundaries of the town, there were no preexistent power strongholds among students. This was true among faculty as well (recruited nationwide in an attempt to match the quality of teaching with the innovative open education approach and design), and also between students and faculty. Twenty percent of both students and faculty were black.

If the customary distribution of power between blacks and whites in our society was to be different in Columbia (and everyone thought that somehow it ought to be different here), it seemed to make sense that blacks might have to take some steps to make it different. That "nigger" and "honkie" were heard in the halls, and that flare-ups of hostility sometimes followed, could therefore have been expected as blacks and whites vied to change or to maintain the distribution of power they were used to in a situation where blacks were still clearly a minority.

This hostility between black and white youth was discussed quietly in the adult community as a "sign of prejudice" and the result of "all different kinds of kids being thrown together in a new high school." This kind of problem would not occur, people said, when "the kids who've grown up, black and white together, get older." There are now young adults in Columbia who have spent most of their elementary school years together; nonetheless, competition and separation in the secondary schools remain. One white teenager reported, "My best friend can't speak to me in the halls without trouble from her black friends."

That race was hardly ever mentioned as a problem in public and rarely in private was contrary to my experience in an inner-city neighborhood, where blacks and whites talked together continually about why so few blacks attended PTA meetings and about how to avoid further white exodus to the suburbs. In Columbia it was only whispered that one of three teen centers was "all black" and that the other two were "becoming black." At the same time, whites saw the federally subsidized housing complexes in Columbia as "80 to 90 percent black," when in fact fewer than 40 percent of the residents of these units were black.

These incongruities began to spark my sociological conscious-ness. Once the research had been funded and was formally under way, each of the five members of the family became a participant observer. One, for example, was in the first class at the high school and in its first graduating class as well. One was an active member of the first men's consciousness-raising group. While I, as the full-time anthro-pologist, spent my days and evenings in a more structured approach to data gathering, the others were continually adding richness to my study—particularly those areas that centered on young adult inter-actions.

Most analysts of a community such as Columbia would have predicted that the lines of fragmentation in this situation of two classes (lower income and middle class) and two races (black and white) would be economic. In other words, middle-class blacks and whites would tacitly agree to pursue common goals and blacks would emphasize their class position over their ethnic identity, as indeed many blacks have done in the past, in order to secure acceptance in racially integrated circumstances. When youth lined up by race across class lines there was great consternation, and explanations about the long-lasting nature of racial prejudice were used by school personnel and parents to try to make sense of this unexpected and unwanted choice of boundary marking.

Middle-class black youth were emphasizing their blackness rather than their middle-class position. Considering the heavy emphasis on racial integration in Columbia, why would black youth have made this choice? The continual effort in the community to deny or ignore this separatist process, and failing this, to attribute it to prejudice with roots outside the Columbia experience, led me to ask what this process among youth might mirror in the adult com-munity.

The findings of this study have important policy implications. Serious questions have been raised about both the fiscal and the social wisdom of building new communities. Further, several large-scale investigations have suggested that the level of satisfaction with the quality of life is not much improved in these communities. Largely hidden within the sophisticated quantitative conclusions of these studies, however, are some intriguing themes: women are more satisfied than men; blacks than whites; owners than renters; those with less formal education than those with more; those with incomes of over $10,000 than those with less.[1]

Unfortunately, in the attempts to generalize about the quality of life in new towns, the responses to standardized questionnaires have been aggregated and manipulated until the fabric of social relationships is submerged in categorical attitudes (that is, categories such as race, gender, age, and the like). These generalizations fail to consider that the expectations for what life ought to be like in this "Next America" and the reality of what is indeed happening daily between residents have considerable bearing on the perceptions that these residents reflect in their responses to interview schedules. Thus, much of the research and reporting about life in new towns unconsciously incorporates these expectations in the questions asked. Perceived problems come to represent failure while reported satisfactions become the keyword of success. Simplistic answers, given to old questions, form the narrative of what it is like to live in a new town; problems are ignored unless they are blatant, and then the problems are taken at face value as signs of failure. The unfortunate result is that the reports of these investigations exhibit a startling failure to capture a sense of community life.

Columbians carry with them both the exuberant expectations and the persistent criticisms that the term "new town" conveys in the United States today. But in between the ideals of the planners and social scientists and the reports of researchers and journalists who write about racial antagonism, class isolation, and a suburban atmosphere, there lies a narrative of community building that incorporates both the dreams of James Rouse and the skepticism of his critics. The story of Columbia is not one of success or failure or of relative perceptions of satisfaction with the quality of life in a new town. Nor will it show conclusively whether new forms of racial and social mixing are possible in the United States, in new towns or elsewhere. It is rather a chronicle of how a stable, plural community has developed within the confines of a social experiment that included, along with innovative programs for land use, education, recreation, and medical and social services, the careful and deliberate inclusion of persons who are poor as well as persons who are black. This story has bearing for race and class relations far beyond a new town environment.

By the mid-1970s Columbia was a community of almost 40,000 people, where eight years before there had been only farms. The story is indeed one of poor and nonpoor, black and white, old and young, married, divorced, and single. The fact that the story must be ferreted out of rhetoric about the uses of physical and social space, recreation habits, property ownership and maintenance, fee schedules, the care of small children, and the lack of care for adolescents, is what makes it an interesting account and one worth telling. While community pluralism is much older than America, it is relatively new as a planned concept.

The problems encountered in making heterogeneous communities work for all residents is not a new one. The gap between the ideology of egalitarianism and equal opportunity and the reality that some people have more prestige and get more rewards than others has generated similar problems in other communities. This means that while the experience of racial and economic mixing in Columbia is important in itself, there are insights of a larger dimension to be drawn from a careful examination of this particular instance. This is especially so in the present period when moves to end racial and socioeconomic discrimination and isolation are becoming more intense.

Columbia allows us to observe these processes of social change with many more pieces of the puzzle available than is normally the case in larger or older communities. The contradictory strains that yield a nation from many different groups and categories of people and at the same time reinforce the integrity of the cultures of these groups are also felt in Columbia. This book is an analysis of these forces in one community.

NOTE

1   Burby and Weiss 1976

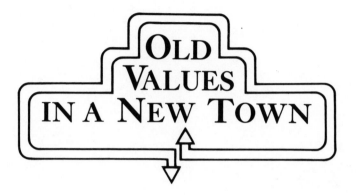

1

ETHNOGRAPHIC
DESCRIPTION
AND SOCIAL ANALYSIS

Columbia seemed an ideal setting in which to look at the structural roots of racial antagonism and class isolation. While seldom applied to political relationships in communities in the United States, anthropology was particularly well suited to the examination of this community where the relationships between two major independent variables, race and class, seemed difficult to sort out. Perhaps the major tenet of an anthropologist is that extraordinary steps must be taken to see that the assumptions of a research question are tested against the experiences of the subject *as he or she views them*. These efforts can bring a fresh perspective to social and political relations in complex situations, particularly in the case where previous assumptions are confounding the investigation by slipping into the research design and questionnaire development. This chapter looks at the connections among the substantive issues of race and class in Columbia, the methods of description and analysis in social anthropology, and the particular theoretical focus within anthropology that I take.

RACE, CLASS, AND A SENSE OF COMMUNITY

As I began to reexamine the conclusions of other investigators of American community life since W. Lloyd Warner's landmark series nearly a half century before, I discovered that almost all these studies of social relations in urban and nonurban situations had found that, whenever race and class were present as organizing vehicles of social relationships in a research setting, class had usually been found to explain the most.[1] That is, most studies have found that when people are faced with a conscious or unconscious choice, they will make decisions or form alliances based on class affiliation. A 1972 advisory report to the U.S. Department of Housing and Urban Development (HUD), for example, reviewed the literature on housing segregation and pointed out that research efforts in this field reveal an overlapping of black and white socioeconomic hierarchies only at equal points on the ladder of prestige (in other words, blacks and whites can only begin to interact in a color-blind manner with each other when their educational or occupational ranks are similar). In this report the committee urged that high priority be given to research programs on the issue of simultaneous racial and socioeconomic mixing in order to create an adequate knowledge base for policies in this area.[2] Nearly a decade later the literature continues to debate the relative weight of these two critical variables with little advance in clarity.[3]

As I looked more closely at the literature on race and class mixing that was available when I formulated the research, it became clear that most of the studies placed undue emphasis on the attitudes of a random set of respondents, and assumed a close, if not causal, connection between attitudes and behavior. For example, the Advisory Committee to HUD reports that while high status whites express more favorable attitudes toward blacks than lower status whites, the higher status whites are more likely to move out of an area that is racially changing.[4] In fact, the findings about the relationship between attitudes and behavior in situations of race and class mixing are contradictory. On the one hand, subtle processes of social change find their way into the behavioral repertoire of individuals long before they are translated into values or attitudes, as in the case where white factory workers develop close relationships with black fellow workers while continuing to espouse the idea that "they should live in their own neighborhoods." On the other hand, attitudes about equal access and the negative effects of discrimination can become common parlance with very little correspondence to actual behavior, as in situations where nondiscrimination clauses are said to be adhered to while the qualifications for the sought after commodity (education, housing, a job) are actually much higher for a minority group member. This suggested that the most important questions in situations where both race and class are significant variables center around this gap between what people profess and what they in fact do.

A good example of this discrepancy between what people say and what they do is the rather large-scale effort that was put into redefining the goals of Columbia as a community in 1973. With the support of the Columbia Association, appointees and volunteers from each village had formulated a set of specific concerns known as the Goals Council Report. This report, while carefully pointing out that it did not seek "to deal with CA goals or objectives, but only its policies," nevertheless directed itself to reporting thoughts of the residents of Columbia about "the role CA should, or can, play in each of sixteen categories of human activity."

A few of these 16 areas generated a lengthy debate at a meeting of all the boards of the four village associations then in existence. It was at this meeting that I first became aware of several controversial issues that were to reappear continually throughout the 18 months of field research. These issues foreshadow the case studies in subsequent chapters: a sliding scale for payment for facility use, commitment to a large expenditure in day care, the problem of teenagers, and residents' property values.

Just as interesting, however, was one of the items that was hardly argued about at all. With little overt enthusiasm and some agreement that this was not an issue for the public domain, but with the urging of one member who said, "We must not deal lightly with this issue; we *do* have race problems in Columbia," this item was adopted:

> The Columbia Association will endeavor to promote community in the sense that Columbia is a community whose members are aware of Columbia's purposes, are concerned for the welfare of each other as members of the community, welcome diversity of life styles and beliefs, deal constructively with conflict, and assume responsibility for the actions of the group.

There is much that is implicit in this statement. The Columbia Association has, or should have, the means to "promote community."

Columbia as a community embodies a set of "purposes" that all residents are aware of. Finally, some kinds of conflict and differences in life-style are present in this town and are not being dealt with "constructively."

Community is just as elusive, perhaps more so, for those who experience it as it is for those who come from outside to seek its dimensions. The social historian may approach the question across the barrier of time, analyzing the records and diaries of members of early intentional communities. The literary analyst may define something like the Bloomsbury Group, and seek an association between the dynamic of commitment between a particular group of writers and the works of literature they produced. Sociologists or anthropologists may use locality as the boundary they must move within in order to begin to understand how the actions of people in a geographical community exhibit some kind of consistency. The student of urban politics may frame the social field conceptually rather than territorially asking, for example, "What are the causes of urban riots?" or "What do blacks want?" and look for community in the nature of ethnicity and political collectivism.

Each approach asks questions about alternate structures of human community, about the process of communicating a system of rights and obligations between groups or categories of people. All face one consistently overriding problem: statements that people make about the criteria for belonging and commitment are generalities, and as such are readily manipulated by them and by others. There are discrepancies between what people adhere to as "right" and their actual behavior when defining what constitutes membership in a community. The flexibility that is present in ideals that people profess about community allows them to deal with the lack of fit between ideology and behavior in a manner that causes as little conflict as possible. This study looks at how people choose between and manipulate such a shared ideology, and does this through the eyes and ears of a social anthropologist.

CULTURAL SYMBOLS AND POLITICAL POWER

Social anthropologists say they study social structures, which is another way of saying they study the systematic organization of social relationships. Social relationships are taken to be abstractions that are very difficult to observe except as patterns of behavior emerge over time, and thus are not readily accessible to the survey questionnaire. Because their structure consists of the ideas individuals have in their heads about "the distribution of power between persons and groups of persons,"[5] anthropologists believe that in order to study social structures one must examine the categories people use to associate or disassociate themselves from others.

All of us share an elaborate system of communicating about social differences. Among the more obvious categories that people use to communicate about who belongs where are class, race, religion, and national origin; gender has always served such a purpose and is of late becoming a powerful political force as well. Sexual preference is another category that is becoming a more open social and political organizer. However, even when the relevance of a category or combination of categories is obvious, Americans sometimes deny that political alliances are based on them. For example, the Right-to-Life movement has expended a great deal of energy and money in the past trying to reduce the public image that it has strong ties to Catholicism (and thus may be "only" a religious organization). The national women's movement strains to avoid being too closely identified with lesbian feminists by openly encouraging more traditionally feminine modes of dress among its visibly active members.

Alternate and elaborate mechanisms are generated as part of our cultural repertoire in order to give us methods of sorting out who belongs where that are as uncontroversial as possible. Erving Goffman is but one of many social scientists who have systematically examined these mechanisms; he is, however, probably the most widely read. Goffman writes about how we symbolically communicate social differences to each other in situations as varying as that of individuals sharing an elevator and of patients and staff members in a mental hospital.[6]

Indeed, individuals have available a wide range of attributes, some of which may be freely chosen such as dress or speech, and some of which, although in a sense more permanent like skin color or gender, may be emphasized or deemphasized in structuring social interaction. Claims to prestige may vary in presentation and interpretation depending on the situation. Interactions may be one-to-one, and thus in some sense private, or may take place in larger groups and in public settings. The goal of all such behavior is political; namely, to make a statement during the interaction about who belongs where, or as it is sometimes put, about affiliation and ultimately about hierarchy. For example, many blacks, while not free to change the color of their skin, may emphasize or deemphasize their blackness with variations in dress, hairstyle, and patterns of speech in order to increase their control in a situation.

All communities are characterized by some sort of ranking system, and investigations of hierarchical power relations in communities have tended to concentrate on major decision makers and the public decisions they make. The question of rank will be approached from a quite different angle in this community study. Each decision will be seen as representing the result of a series of maneuverings that individuals carry out with the cultural baggage they have at their disposal.

Abner Cohen says, "All behavior, whether in formal or in informal groups, is largely couched in symbolic forms."[7] I am concerned with the symbolism of power relationships and, in particular, with how the system of social stratification is expressed and in the process maintained or changed through relationships between informal political groupings. I have tried to abstract from observed formal and informal interactions the shared understandings individuals hold about the symbols that organize the structure of their daily social universe in Columbia, and then to examine how individuals and groups use these symbols to maintain, convey, and grasp power. In other words, there are two possible stages in the mobilization of symbols: first, the individual's utilization of commonly understood symbols of social status to buttress or improve one's own position vis-a-vis another individual; and second, the manipulation of these symbols to gain or strengthen power positions for a category of individuals. Both of these functions show how the informal system of shared understandings about which symbols to use on which occasions can form the underpinning of informal political action.

We must begin by posing a series of questions. What are the behavioral clues that allow individuals to place themselves inside or outside another's social space? Is there indeed a common understanding of what these clues signal in terms of category allocation? Is this common understanding sometimes at variance with what the word or words would seem to mean, and if so, what part of the process is served by this mystification? Are some of these clues more easily displayed and discussed in public, more socially acceptable? If so, do these clues become covers for the less palatable ones? Further, do all who participate in this use understand and accept that, for example, discussions about the advantages inherent in owned as opposed to rental housing units in an area represent an expression of fear that renters will be of a lower class?

These issues reflect a question of broader significance; namely, how do people communicate with each other about social status? The disconcerting gap between the empirical facts of rank and status and the normative scheme by which people make order of the social world that surrounds their lives is generally lamented in the social sciences. However, it is this intersection between behavior and attitudes or beliefs that needs attention precisely because of the seeming inconsistencies and overlaps. Isolating the ways that people in one community deal with these discrepancies between the empirical and the normative order constitutes a rudimentary step in this direction. By careful examination of when and how individuals employ the major symbols for the communication of who belongs where in one community, I will lay the groundwork from which to argue that because these symbols are imprecise, they can be manipulated to foster a process of gradual and orderly social change that causes no more disruption to the power structure than it can contain.[8]

The ideology of participatory democracy that is widely promulgated and accepted in this community has provided a rich source of data for the isolation of status categories and the symbols that are used to express them. Decision making at all levels is open to public participation; what has been more important for the research effort, it is open to public scrutiny. It was relatively effortless to gain access to countless sessions where arguments about rights and obligations incorporated these status categories. The public record, in terms of minutes of meetings and newspaper articles, is a less reliable but abundant and acceptable source of these kinds of data. Thus, the concern here is with symbols that organize confrontation in public rather than in more casual, one-to-one interactions, and in issues that reflect more the distribution of status in terms of how the pie is divided rather than in issues that reflect how individuals sort out and secure positions vis-a-vis others in their neighborhoods or jobs.

The collective concern of social anthropologists has been the analysis of social relations in the context of culture. While concentrating on the economic, political, kinship, and ritual institutions of the less complex societies, social anthropologists analyze how certain customs both reflect and affect the social hierarchy. Perhaps more clearly stated, we are ultimately interested in the interdependence of culture and social structure. Culture provides the form of social interaction, and as such offers important clues to the underlying structural patterns.

Cultural anthropologists and other social scientists often seek document how people are different. That is to say, they often see the documentation of different ways of life as the subject of research rather than only as an important, although perhaps the most important, clue to social relationships. Many studies of lower income families in American society take the former approach; the "culture of poverty" concept, so widely debated in recent years, is an example. This type of focus can be viewed as a cultural model of ethnicity, focusing attention on customs and distinctive traits and leading to the identification of a group by the attitudes, values, and ideas that are taken as determining what that group "is." This encourages attention to cultural rather than structural aspects of groups, and thus minimizes or overlooks the political functions these attributes serve. In early 1975 a small group of American Indians in South Boston, who seemingly had abandoned their cultural traits in an assimilation process, chose to emphasize their heritage in order to avoid the court-ordered busing program for whites. This vignette exemplifies the struggle for control, at least over one's own life, that is reflected when individuals tailor their public image with the use of symbols in ways that customary analyses based on cultural traits will not explain.

I take the view that symbols are the raw materials that individuals use to maneuver their way through varying kinds of hierarchical situations where the ideology that is professed and the reality of power relationships are not in line with each other. Thus, when people use a phrase such as *lower income* or *middle class* in these sorts of circumstances, they are representing in symbolic form their experiences of power and prestige in their membership groups, or, more precisely, in the categories with which they wish to be affiliated or disassociated.

Elizabeth Bott has suggested that in doing this, the individual is constructing and using reference groups that are formed from multifaceted social experiences both past and present, and defines reference group as:

> any group, real or fictitious, thought by an individual to have a real existence and employed by him to compare or evaluate his position with that of others, and to justify or explain his actions.[9]

It is difficult to identify the relevant reference groups, as Bott and others have referred to them, for the organization of social relationships in a particular social setting. Coping with problems of identification is well worth the effort, however, because this approach avoids a description that assumes that categories such as the poor, blacks, the middle class, and so on are groups with defined boundaries and predictable behavior. If, indeed, differences between socio-economic and racial groups are used for informal political maneuverings in Columbia, an analysis of the relationship between the actual differences and the symbolic manipulation of these differences in the maintenance and redistribution of social power is important to any understanding of the political arena.

The works of two eminent scholars in social anthropology have been critical to this analysis of informal political maneuverings in Columbia. Edmuch Leach discusses social change among the hill peoples in Burma in the following manner:

> In situations such as we find in the Kachin Hills Area, any particular individual can be thought of as having a status position in several different social systems at one and the same time. To the individual himself such systems present themselves as alternatives or inconsistencies in the scheme of values by which he orders his life. The overall process of structural change comes about through the manipulation of these alternatives as a means of social advancement. Every individual of a society, each in his own interest, endeavours to exploit the situation as he perceives it and in so doing the collectivity of individuals alter the structure of the society itself.[10]

Leach further points out that every social system maintains a set of ideas that is ambiguous but nevertheless sufficiently understood by the members of the society, and with which the gap between the ideology about the distribution of power and the empirical reality of rank and privilege is mediated. The key to understanding the informal political process of sorting into "we" and "they" categories that is served through the use of symbols lies in their flexibility and ambiguity, he says, and further refines his focus in *Highland Burma* as "a study of how particular structures can assume a variety of cultural interpretations and how different structures can be represented by the same set of cultural symbols."[11]

The association between Leach's work and Abner Cohen's work is evident when we compare Leach's statement above with the following question posed by Cohen: "What is the range of variation in the symbolic *forms* that perform the same symbolic *function* in political contexts under different cultural traditions?"[12] In a later work, Cohen discusses modern day Chinese society to stress the complementary point that "changes in the relationships of power are often effected by means of symbolic continuities, not by means of new symbolic forms."[13] Reminding the reader of the well-documented political functions of ancestors' cults as part of the traditional complex lineage structures, he points to the communist government's channeling of this symbolic form (ancestor worship) to "what may well be the most massive cult of the dead in history,"[14] that is, the mausoleum to Mao and all its attendant rites and services. Relationships of power, significantly changed by the Chinese revolution, are still buttressed as in former times with symbols that deal with the dead.

Cohen often refers to the relevance he feels his theoretical approach has for the study of social change: "One of the major functions of symbols is to give tangible relatively enduring objectification to relations that are perennially in the process of 'becoming'."[15] The case studies in this book will make clear the connection between the works of Leach and Cohen in understanding social change. The analysis will show that symbols carry the weight of the dialectic between the ideal system of status relations and the informal power among persons in a society. To use class as an example again, our highly stratified society corresponds rather badly with our ideology as an egalitarian nation. The ideology places constraints on an open approach to sorting and hierarchy, and symbols are invented to allow a system of communication about who belongs where to be carried out with as little damage to the ideology as possible. Moreover, these symbols can be reinterpreted to encourage gradual changes in the beliefs or relative position of a person or a sector of the population. Cohen also says that "it is this ambiguity in their meaning that forges symbols into such powerful instruments in the hands of leaders and of groups in mystifying people for particularistic or universalistic or both purposes."[16] Thus I argue that in Columbia a process of "becoming" in Cohen's terms, or "overall structural change" in Leach's terms, is fostered with the use of symbols as covers for the reality of political manipulation.

To summarize, communicating about social differences is the backbone of the informal power order in our society and can be observed in a highly complex system of symbols used in everyday interactions. These symbols have two aspects: first, they take on a form that is to some degree obvious, as when cultural differentiations are emphasized; and second, they have a function that is often less clear. Because form is more easily perceived than function, a great deal of attention has been paid to the markers of cultural differentiation in our society, while the use of cultural markers as vehicles for political collectivism has often been ignored.

I chose to investigate the relationship between cultural symbols and politics in Columbia precisely because of the racial and socio-economic mix. Very much aware of the difficulties of ferreting out these kinds of hidden meanings in a cultural milieu to which one belongs, I nevertheless felt that the planned social change incorporated in the ideology of Columbia would result in a broader range of behaviorial choices for certain categories of people and a richer source of data than might be available in other communities.

METHODS AND EXPLANATION IN SOCIAL ANTHROPOLOGY

We can now return to the assertion that anthropology is well suited to the task of looking at the articulation of race and class in one community, and relate that idea to the theoretical focus of the study just set forth. In other words, how does the central thesis of the book relate to anthropological methods of data collection and analysis?

While it is true that much of an anthropologist's analysis takes place after leaving the field situation, when there is sufficient time and distance to ponder the patterns and connections in the data, the questions that organize what one does while in the field are equally important. The categories of the discipline and the particular theoretical focus of the researcher continually filter what is seen and heard and direct how time is spent. This means, first of all, that the relationship between the methods used to gather data and the process of explanation cannot reasonably be separated into the traditional dichotomy of methods and theory.

This approach is not radically different from that of more quantitatively oriented social scientists who gather data from a random set of respondents based on a set of theoretical assumptions, and then in the privacy of their studies or computer laboratories puzzle through the clues that will allow them to ask further questions of those data. It is, however, quite different from the commonly held assumption that anthropologists employ one method, participant observation, through which they are said to record a myriad of ethnographic detail about a "whole culture" or about one social situation. I am often asked to speak to classes in related disciplines about the methods of anthropology. Each time I am surprised to find that students (and faculty, for that matter) expect a handy list of tools that can be applied in the qualitative study of a community or a group of people. They are dismayed to find that we must begin with a body of data and deal with a set of theoretical assumptions before methods have meaning. Thus, methods in social anthropology reflect both technical and analytic concerns, and these concerns are inextricably linked through the mutually dependent processes of description and analysis.[17]

My initial interest in Columbia was to establish how the presence of various social categories (blacks, whites, middle class, lower income) would affect the way decisions were made. Working in an anthropological framework means that this question makes several assumptions. One of these is that a concentration on isolating the major decision makers and documenting the public decisions taken in a community leaves untouched too many aspects of the question, "Who governs?" Decisions made in the public domain represent considerably more than the culmination of the power plays between major and obvious factions in a community. Rather, each decision represents an endless series of maneuvers that are hidden in at least two ways: first, much negotiation takes place before and after the public airing of a conflict; and second, the public argument is often worded in such a way that the contested resources, and even at times the contenders, are obscured.

Columbia is an ideal site for the investigation of the informal negotiations that surround political decisions because of three characteristics of the community. First, Columbia was built on the foundation of integration of different kinds of people. Second, there remains a heavy emphasis on the idea of equal access for all residents to the resources of the community. This powerful ethic, combined with the third characteristic, a quasi-governmental structure modeled on participatory democracy, results in a continual public debate about issues surrounding this heterogeneity. Columbia thus offers a rich source of data on the alternatives that individuals choose when they attempt to maintain or change their position or that of others in the social hierarchy.

This ethic of participatory democracy encourages endless public meetings. I was able to isolate issues of greater or lesser conflict and follow them over the period of the research, both in terms of discussions in the public eye and private negotiations to which I had access. Continual attendance at one or more meetings each weekday evening was one of the most important methods of uncovering a patterning in the hidden language people use in social situations. This type of activity was important in another sense: it allowed me, in a way that was not threatening to the subjects of the research, to identify both the outlines of the obvious power configurations in the community and the kinds of issues that arose again and again as the subject of discussion and dispute.

This fostered three further sources of information. First, connections between the major actors and the controversial issues could be drawn. The obvious decision makers in a community do not operate in a vacuum; rather, it is a matter of the success of an interest group in establishing itself as a source of legitimacy to those who formally make the decisions. Second, it offered a relatively effortless source of deciding how and where to direct attention outside the organizational setting. Watching and listening to countless interactions between major decision makers and between these decisions makers and their constituencies allowed efficient direction of casual interviewing outside the organizational setting. Moreover, it helped me learn to cut through obscuring rhetoric in ways that never would have been possible without the general understanding of the issues that resulted from faithful attendance at these meetings. Third, and critical from a methodological standpoint, my presence in the rear of these meetings taking notes every night, for weeks and months, engendered a confidence in my genuine interest in the community that proved invaluable. The research activity was openly discussed with anyone who expressed an interest, and a considerable degree of trust was carefully established. Developing and maintaining a reciprocal relationship with people in the community is a part of this trust and required a heavy time investment. Legends about anthropologists providing cigarettes and antibiotics in remote places are common; in Columbia there is nothing with which to reciprocate except the time of the investigator. This meant serving on noncontroversial committees and boards of directors, providing editing services, advising on demographic analyses, and listening patiently. As it became clear that I was not interested in jumping to conclusions about sensational and divisive issues, a network of informants was spontaneously generated.

Most of my days were spent following the network of informants around the community. For example, each evening a choice had to be made about which meeting might prove most useful for the research. Because of their trust and interest in what I was doing, individuals would phone with tips about what was expected to occur at a particular meeting, with information about something I had missed the previous day, and with invitations to sit in on behind-the-scenes negotiations.

Both types of activity discussed above—observation in organizational settings and selective informal interviewing around the community—were critical in insuring the reliability and the validity of my approach. Observation in organizational settings allowed me to have confidence that the data gathered in these situations had the reliability of naturally occurring behavior, while the continuity of my approach over 18 months meant I could reduce the risk of misinterpreting the relevance of behaviors observed in these meetings. On the other hand, following the network of information that emerged was critical to understanding the significance of what was *not* said in public and the types of agreements that were made between participants before and after the public airing of an issue.

The problem of trust and access in qualitative studies of community decision making raises a further methodological device employed early in the research effort. Although I had been a resident of Columbia for two years prior to this time, it seemed wise to move to a new location as the research became more formalized in order to avoid the possibility of presuming on neighborhood friendships formed before the nature of my research was established. Two issues figure prominently in the eventual choice of neighborhood. First, because I sought to investigate the intersection between issues of race and class, I considered it important to look for a neighborhood where blacks and whites, as well as middle class and lower income, were present in relatively close proximity. Racial integration of housing is completely successful in Columbia, making the choice a simple one when only race was a consideration. Subsidized housing, however, while scattered on various sites throughout the community, is somewhat more difficult to live close to. We eventually purchased an attached house in a complex of 88 such homes just under construction immediately adjacent to one of the five sites of Interfaith Housing, a federally subsidized complex of 45 apartments and townhouses in the village of Wilde Lake.*

At the time I viewed the decision to move into the new development of moderate priced attached houses as a unique opportunity to observe social relationships in a socioeconomically mixed setting at close hand. However, very little took place in this mixed neighborhood that could in any way be viewed as resulting from the economic mix. The formation of friendships and the expression of minor irritations were similar to those observed in neighborhoods not populated by such a wide mixture of residents. This can be viewed as a finding in itself given the opposition that often surfaces when construction of subsidized housing in a neighborhood is proposed.

The second reason for choosing this neighborhood is also important. As anyone who has moved into a newly constructed subdivision will attest, residents in this situation are relatively open in their neighborliness as they seek to establish a sense of place about their new homes. Moreover, problems of faulty construction engender difficulties between the residents and the builder that provide a natural bond between these new residents. This means that, while middle-class Americans can be rather careful and private in neighborly interactions, under conditions such as these there is an opportunity to observe considerably more in the way of social interaction patterns. Having decided to look at how power is maintained and grasped by categories of people in this community, my target group was the visible elites, for the most part professional, well educated, and solidly middle class. Choosing this neighborhood provided me with firsthand knowledge of a small subset of such Columbia residents.

I faced at least two further hurdles. Most microsociological investigations of informal political groupings such as I proposed to carry out have been conducted in other cultures where the anthropologist's own cultural repertoire is quite different from the one to be studied. Although mastering a foreign language and learning the customs of an alien group are difficult, the strange nuances become important clues that are not available in one's own milieu. As a

---

*The history and organizational structure of the Columbia Interfaith Housing Corporation is discussed at some length in Chapter 6.

member of the group that was the subject of the research, it was to some extent necessary to laboriously unlearn what certain phrases meant in order not to miss these clues. At the same time, in order to foster an air of legitimacy and thus insure my access to information other than that available in the public domain, I had to understand the cultural nuances very well.

Second, while studies of this type have been carried out in Western societies, much of the work has centered on, for example, ethnic groups, youth groups, poor people, and poor blacks; in other words, on less powerful minorities. There is little guidance to be found in previous studies for exploring the association between power among elites in the United States and the symbolism that is used to maintain that power. It is difficult to examine the exercise of power unless one has some handle on the more or less invisible groups that are contending for resources, yet the right to privacy that accrues to middle-class elites confounds understanding what the threats to their power are. Cohen suggests one reason for this:

> The more privileged a group is in society the more secretive and mystifying it tends to be about its organization and strategies. This does not mean that members of these groups consciously and deliberately use the symbolism of concealment and mystification in a brazen utilitarian manner. Often what might have been at first a symbolic performance staged to mystify outsiders is unconsciously adopted by the performers as an end in itself, convincing themselves, as much as the outsiders, of the validity of their symbolic formations and ideology.[18]

As I continued my observation of the obvious political actors in the decision-making process, and heightened my participation in noncontroversial roles within the system, some areas of interface between the target group and other categories in the community began to emerge. It became very clear that the patience needed for continued attendance at public meetings was more than worth the effort because of the rich resource that dispute and conflict offered when they arose.

Sally Moore has pointed to the ethnographic usefulness of following a dispute process:

> The dispute between individuals that expands provides both a specific *occasion* for confrontation and a set of concrete, self-justifying *terms* in which the confrontation can be thought of and discussed [emphasis in original].[19]

In the same passage she discusses an inherent problem with dispute analysis:

> . . . when, as in law, there is what appears to be a rational connection between the reasons given for social action and the action itself, it is sometimes more difficult to analyze the relationship among the rationalizations, the actions, and their setting.[20]

Moore's warning is well-taken, and calls for precisely the sort of integration between method (in this case, long-term observation of the rise of and negotiations accompanying conflict situations) and analysis (that is, explanation of what is observed that adheres to a theoretical focus that guides the observer to see patterns in the data) that marks the discipline of social anthropology.

As we move in the chapters ahead through a series of conflicts that were observed in the public arena and that uncover negotiations for power that take place between different categories of people in this heterogeneous community, important connections will be shown to exist between these groups and the symbols that allow the manipulation of power to remain largely covert. First, though, we must take a brief look at the physical, social, and political characteristics of the setting from which these observations have been drawn.

NOTES

1	Warner and Lunt 1941
2	Advisory Committee 1972:56
3	Vincent 1978
4	Advisory Committee 1972:9
5	Leach 1954:4
6	Goffman 1959; 1961
7	Cohen 1969:228
8	Leach 1954
9	Bott 1971:165
10	Leach 1954:8
11	Leach 1954:279
12	Cohen 1974:33
13	Cohen 1979:104
14	Cohen 1979:93
15	Cohen 1969:217
16	Cohen 1979:103
17	Fortes 1970:129
18	Cohen 1974:110
19	Moore 1972:97
20	Moore 1972:97

2

AUTHORITY, LEGITIMACY, AND POWER

A MODEL FOR THE NEXT AMERICA

Columbia was one of the earliest new towns in the United States. The first residents arrived in 1967 with feelings not unlike those of earlier frontier breakers: excitement, worry about the economic soundness of their decision, fear of a new way of life, and a pressing need to share with others the good and the bad of this new experience. These early residents had a strong sense of themselves as pioneers, responsible for laying the foundation on which a new kind of community life would be built.

Their enthusiasm was understandable, for Columbia had a national reputation as part of the popular new town movement that flourished under both private and public sponsorship in the late 1960s and early 1970s. Born out of the raging debates about our sick and dying cities and our anonymous, burgeoning suburbs, this movement embodied enthusiastic ideas about how life could be improved through innovative use of physical resources and planning of social institutions. Columbia, as one of the first models of this utopian scheme, was designed to provide a range of employment and recreational opportunities, convenient shopping facilities, and an exceptionally broad choice in style and price of housing clustered in ways that would foster social bonds around neighborhood schools to which each child could walk.

The most unusual goal, however, was to furnish these opportunities to as many different kinds of people as possible. The new town vision of James Rouse has become known as "a garden for growing people." Indeed, the logo of the city, depicted in a large bronze structure at the lakefront in the town center, shows people with arms stretched upward, growing from a common base. Central to this idea that people grow through contact with other kinds of people is the conviction that racial and class isolation (one-class suburbs in particular) are destructive to the development of healthy community life. Convinced that the building block of heterogeneity was absent in suburban complexes and threatened or completely destroyed in blighted urban areas, Rouse held firmly to the notion that in order to foster the kinds of social relationships upon which a sense of community would develop, it was essential to provide for a racial and socioeconomic mix.

As he carefully and quietly gathered land on which to build this new city, planners and social scientists sought to articulate the dream into a set of explicit goals. These goals are abstracted from early documents and reified anew each year when Rouse joins with other residents to celebrate Columbia's birthday. The assertion that Columbia fosters human growth in a complete and balanced community that is concerned about ecology, good design, and economic viability paraphrases the annual renewal statement. Most important to the guiding ideology is the concept of a well-rounded city with a wide diversity in its population. Age, race, and class were the critical markers of diversity sought after, and the rhetoric surrounding this ideology has become an integral component of the spoken and unspoken expectations about the quality of life in this new community.

A SENSE OF PLACE

The efforts to fashion a sense of community are reflected in the physical layout as well. Without the set of expectations that goes with knowing that Columbia is a new town, a visitor might report some of these visual impressions. Housing, while at times reminiscent of an average new suburb, is more varied in style and is clustered to leave more open space. The pattern of winding, tree-lined streets on the hilly terrain reduces the sense of row upon row of new homes. Property fencing, overhead wiring, television antennas, clotheslines, and large advertising signs are absent, and public buildings and businesses seem to meld comfortably with the other structures and with the landscape. Only a few main streets lead anywhere but into a residential cul-de-sac, thus restricting traffic on most residential streets to those who live there. The commercial and recreational centers appear busy, and unlike a suburban community some miles outside the central business district of a large city, benches, stores, and restaurants are filled at midday with men and women, dressed in both casual and business clothes.

Columbia is situated between the Washington and Baltimore metropolitan areas, and covers approximately one-tenth of semirural Howard County, or about 15,000 acres.* The first residents moved to Columbia in 1967. The population at the time of this research was approximately 40,000, and is expected to double by 1985 when the community should be fully developed. While formally within the governmental jurisdiction of Howard County, it is distinguished from the rest of the county by zoning regulations, and is autonomous in the areas of early childhood education, recreation, and transportation services. Columbia in 1975 was a predominately white, middle-class community, although it had achieved an unusual racial and class diversity. The population at that time was 20 percent black; 15 percent of all residents earned less than $10,000 annually, with average annual income for both blacks and whites nearing $20,000.

The physical plan of the new town is made up of seven villages of two to five residential neighborhoods, each surrounding a large commercial and office center. Twenty percent of the total land area has been set aside for open space, and a variety of recreational amenities have been provided. Two golf courses, indoor and outdoor tennis courts and swimming pools, an indoor skating rink, and an

---

*Howard County, Maryland, is located in the southwestern portion of the Baltimore SMSA and is bordered by Carroll County to the north, Baltimore and Anne Arundel counties to the east, Prince George's County to the south, and Montgomery and Frederick counties to the west. According to the 1970 U.S. census count, this mainly rural and residential county had a population of 61,911 persons.

athletic club are among these, as well as miles of bicycle and hiking paths, and boating and fishing on three recreational lakes. Elementary schools are located at the core of each neighborhood, and land is provided to the county in each village for middle and high schools. Basic shopping and service facilities are provided at retail centers located in each village; there were four village centers at the time of the research.

Housing reflects a variety of styles and formats as well as a wide range in cost. In 1975 there were condominiums starting at $20,500, townhouses available in the $40,000 to $55,000 range, and single family homes from $50,000 to well over $100,000. Apartments in federally subsidized lower income units rented for approximately $150 a month, depending on family income in some units and on the size of the unit in others. Larger, privately owned townhouse and luxury apartment rental complexes were, of course, much more expensive. The commitment of the developer to devote 20 percent of new town land to business and industry was reflected in three industrial parks under development, and the General Electric Company was developing a 1,000 acre appliance park on the south-eastern fringe of the city.

If one walks and drives around Columbia and glances through a summary of the physical and demographic plans that are directing development, it is clear that Columbia has been planned to provide employment, recreation, convenient shopping facilities, an exceptionally broad range of housing, a pleasing physical environment, and a racial and class mix. This, however, tells little about what it is like to live in the community.

People in Columbia talk about the need for a social model. They contrast this idea with that of the Columbia economic model, updated and shared several times a year with residents, and spelling out in some detail how the resident's money is being used by the Columbia Association. Underlying the conception of a social model is a set of expectations about life in this town where it was hoped that all different kinds of people would want to join together to forge a new kind of community. "Join together" incorporates a myriad of ideas about public, private, political, and social behaviors. Many of these become clearer when we look at the problems residents talk about privately.

There is no sense of neighborhood, they say; people do not draw their friends from within neighborhood boundaries, and do not come out to support or argue about neighborhood issues. Some categories of residents, specifically apartment dwellers and blacks, are not involved in making decisions. Lower income residents feel stigmatized. Subsidized housing is thought to be almost all black. Blacks and whites, particularly young adults, isolate themselves from one another socially, and rumors about incidents of verbal and physical hostility are heard. It is said that these kinds of incidents increased with the opening of subsidized housing, although many concede that young adults from all income levels are involved. Almost all programs for teenagers have followed a path from integrated usage to nearly all-black participation to cancellation. Most decision-making positions in the community are held by whites. "Outsiders from Washington and Baltimore" fish around the lakes, and the "wrong ages of children" use the tot-lots and open spaces near some residents' homes. These allusions to problems express implicitly an uneasiness that is much less frequently expressed openly: will the black population grow to exceed the "comfortable" 20 percent?

Whether or not any of these assertions is true, it may be useful to see them as an expression of the anxiety that often accompanies integration by race or income level. One must be a careful listener in order to have access to open expressions of problems, for such statements are hardly ever made publicly in Columbia. The dominant ideology calls for racial and class integration. It is in the nature of any ideology, however, that it must remain largely unexamined; what people say they want, what they argue about and are willing to mobilize for, what they choose to spend their money on, and what they worry about are important pieces of the puzzle.

In order to grasp the connections between the individual and corporate actors who will emerge in the cases that follow, a discussion of the authority structure and how it operates is a necessary background. Even more important is to establish the link between the manipulation of the ideals of community sketched out above and the intricacies of Columbia's quasi-governmental structure. Because the planners of Columbia envisioned a local system of participatory democracy and carefully set up a hierarchy of bodies designed to incorporate residents in the making of decisions, it is possible to observe and record the choices people make in concert with the rhetoric in which the choices are framed. In other words, we can watch what people do and listen to the reasons they give for what they do. This in a sense allows us to see the gap between ideology and behavior. Moreover, the ideology of equality, so important to this community, is used to contest quite different resources than the rhetoric suggests.

The relationship between authority and power is approached in the following manner: formal statements about the way the local decision-making system is supposed to work are taken as the structure of authority. Such statements about the functions of the various parts of Columbia's governance system, however, reveal very little about how decisions are actually made and carried out. This points to the importance of sources of legitimacy as a necessary component of power. Power is defined here as the ability of an individual, group, or category of persons to institute, influence, or carry out policies in a direction that reflects self-interest. This may indicate competition over either objective or subjective resources. The succeeding chapters show that the withholding of, and fight for, a certain material resource often mirrors a competition for increased respect or prestige. The exercise of power, either in making or influencing actions that affect collectivities of persons, is dependent on the successful manipulation of sources of legitimacy. These sources are available to those who hold positions of formal authority and those who do not. However, a position of authority that is not carefully buttressed by attention to potential sources of legitimacy is often an empty prize.

THE FORMAL ORGANIZATION OF LOCAL GOVERNMENT

When it became clear to the early planners of this new town that political autonomy could not be wrested from Howard County, and when faced with the reality of building an innovative community with superior services and facilities within the confines of a tradition-bound, rural, and financially conservative county system of government, the Columbia Association* was designed and incorporated

> to build, operate, and maintain facilities, services, and amenities over and above those normally provided by the county government,

---

*This organization was incorporated as the Columbia Parks and Recreation Association. The informal but pervasive change to the Columbia Association is taken as an indication of the increased scope of activities that are now a part of the association's regular affairs. Almost everyone uses simply CA in even the most formal settings.

with the goal of creating the highest possible quality urban living environment, and . . . to serve as a channel for the energy and resources of the community in building a new quality of community life.[1]

The financial soundness of this organization is largely based on a continuing first lien, placed in the deed to each piece of taxable property and obligating the owner to pay an annual assessment to the Columbia Association in the amount of $.75 for each $100 of assessed value. These revenues serve as security for the money the organization borrows for its construction expenses, while the fees charged for the use of major recreation facilities and certain programs go mostly for operating costs. To give an idea of the amount of financial resources that CA manages, in fiscal year 1975 the proposed total spending level of the corporation was just under $7 million. The competition for and allocation of these monies represent an enormous task that faces CA for six months of every year, and generate much open conflict and debate in the community about priorities and goals for the future.

Each new resident to Columbia is introduced to the purposes and responsibilities of membership in the association through a handbook published by CA staff and distributed by the real estate companies that operate in the community. The prevalent description of CA as a "permanent community institution" attempts to educate residents about the ideology of Columbia, the responsibilities of management, and their own rights and responsibilities as Columbia citizens:

> In addition to the facilities the Columbia Association owns and operates, and the numerous services and programs it conducts, CA is something more. It is a permanent Columbia institution, dedicated to community purposes, which possesses very substantial economic, physical, and human resources. One of the most important things about CA is that it will be an enduring community-controlled institution which Columbia residents can use to provide the services and opportunities they consider important, to design programs, to construct facilities and amenities, to deal with problems, and to plan for the future. Of all the steps—and there were many—that Jim Rouse took to make Columbia a new town in the far reaching social and community sense, the creation of CA may well stand out in the future as the most important and the most enduring. No one knows what roles Columbia's residents will determine for CA in the next century. The residents could

decide to have CA reduce recreation and athletic programs in favor of wide ranging programs in the fine arts; the residents could decide to use some of CA's revenues to guarantee the development of housing for low-income families, or they could decide to develop coffee houses, nature centers, public gardens, or beer joints. The point is that in the 21st Century CA will be here and Columbia's residents will have this institution, with its substantial resources, to respond to community needs and purposes.

The task today is to devote our best efforts and judgment to the continuing process of developing CA's capabilities in order to prepare CA and the community for the time, which is not far off, when CA will be controlled by the elected representatives of the community serving on the Columbia Association's Board of Directors. Each year of CA's growth is crucial to its development as a community institution—a viable, responsive organization which continually adapts to new problems and seizes new opportunities.[2]

The highest governing body of the Columbia Association is its board of directors, which meets quarterly; a more active role is taken by the executive committee, a subcommittee of the board of directors that meets every two months.* The articles of incorporation provide for a phasing process whereby the representatives appointed by the developer, the Howard Research and Development Corporation (or HRD, a division of the Rouse Company), are gradually reduced while the representatives chosen by the community increase, based on Columbia's growth rate. During most of the research period the executive committee was composed of four developer representatives holding one vote each and five elected members of the community entitled to one-half vote for each 2,000 dwelling units (at that time, 10,000). It was estimated in 1973-74 that, beginning in 1981, CA would be governed entirely by men and women elected from the community. These community representatives are commonly referred to as council reps, reflecting the establishment in the articles of the Columbia Council, a body in name only at present, but designed to include one member elected from each of Columbia's villages, who would then nominate from among their membership the appropriate number of candidates to serve on the board of directors and the executive committee based upon the stage of development.

---

*In response to community pressure, both bodies changed their policy from closed to open sessions just prior to the initiation of the research.

The Columbia Association staff is directed by a president who is appointed by the board of directors. Except for matters of corporate policy and budget approval (the responsibility of the board of directors and its executive committee), the president and the association's key management personnel make the operational decisions for the corporation. The president sits on the board without voting privilege because Maryland law requires the chief executive officer of a corporation to be a member of that corporation's board of directors. Overall financial planning, legal matters, and other administrative responsibilities are also handled by the office of the president.

The distinction between these two facets of the Columbia Association (the executive committee and the administrative staff) should be emphasized because it helps clarify the vulnerability of CA staff that will emerge later in this chapter. The staff administrates a multimillion dollar corporation at the direction of the executive committee, while at the same time serving the members of the association—the residents of Columbia. The executive committee is still dominated by the developer, which means that the elected council reps are not yet in a position to fully represent Columbia's citizens in that role; that is, they can be outvoted by the HRD appointees. Thus, CA staff must balance two somewhat disparate sources of legitimacy, the executive committee and the residents. It is important to understand that the actions of CA staff can never be wholly separate from the influence of the executive committee, and by virtue of numerical dominance, from the developer.

All owners of property and tenants who reside under written lease in one of Columbia's villages are automatically members of that village association. When a unit is owned or leased by more than one member, such members are collectively entitled to only one vote in village elections. The articles of incorporation for each village provide for an association board of directors of five persons, commonly known as the village board. These members are elected annually, and meet in public session bimonthly to consider the business of the association. Residents must petition in advance if they wish to address themselves to an item on the agenda of a particular meeting, although most village boards include a short period of time for residents to speak out before the board at each meeting.

The business of village boards is varied and voluminous. These bodies are designed to be the vehicle through which the concerns of residents are transmitted to policymakers. The result is that a village board must serve as a forum for the interests of individual residents and for organized groups in the village, as well as deal with the everyday concerns and administrative business that are part of handling the affairs of a village of eight to ten thousand residents. Thus, although the village boards function in an advisory role to CA rather than as autonomous policymaking bodies, they have the potential to influence policy because of their structural position in relation to the source of legitimacy that citizen interest groups can represent. Village board issues arise again and again in the following chapters for this reason, and some of the conflicts inherent in having such an important source of legitimacy without a clear vehicle for exercising the power that this could offer will become clear.

INVISIBLE SOURCES OF LEGITIMACY

There are significant resources available to individuals or groups through which they can force attention and action on their needs and desires, and the Columbia Association must maneuver around these invisible pockets of power. How do these collectivities engender questions about the legitimacy of CA's authority, and what kind of a potential threat does this constitute?

One such source of potential power is the category of property owner. The political domain is scarcely entered by those who do not own property. In fact, because property owner is a status category that covertly rules out other unmentionable categorizations (unemployed, for example), many power confrontations use the symbols of property ownership. Home ownership may be a more important symbol in Columbia than it is in the larger society; numerous individuals have commented that social stratification on the basis of type of tenure and type of dwelling unit (in particular, lower status for apartment dwellers) is more pronounced in Columbia than it is in the metropolitan areas in which they formerly resided. This has not gone unnoticed by the Columbia Association, nor has it failed to note that apartment dwellers (and townhouse residents as well) are considerably less satisfied with living in Columbia than single-family homeowners.[3] This categorization and alienation constitute a problem for CA as it seeks to ensure the legitimization of its authority.

On the one hand, then, the political domain as represented by the formal organizational structure (and in particular, the elected representatives of each village) is largely populated by property owners. A recalcitrant village board can be a painful thorn in the side of CA, for there are often instances where village boards constitute the most needed resource of legitimacy for CA. Since renters rarely run for elected position, CA's most important legitimators turn out to be middle-class property owners, carrying with them a strong orientation to emphasize property values. This means, of course, that the interests of the CA executive commitee (and to some extent CA staff) and elected citizens dovetail very nicely; both tend to be more concerned with the financial and aesthetic health of the community than with the kinds of social concerns that apartment dwellers, some of whom barely manage to be financially solvent and many of whom are single parents, might reflect.

On the other hand, CA is aware that any dissatisfied category of resident has the potential to make demands on the system. Even though there has been little sign of disruption from apartment dwellers, the concern about the potential threat is great enough to encourage a flow of rhetoric about "integrating apartment dwellers into the community," and periodically to elicit proposals to study the needs of apartment dwellers.

Blacks and lower income residents are both categories with a great deal of potential power. Columbia's ideology about the importance of racial and socioeconomic mixing plays an intriguing role here. While encouraging public attention to areas where the ideology is undermined by the facts, it simultaneously tends to keep issues surrounding race and class as hidden agendas because of the constraints on categorizing either part of the population freely. The local press manages to keep CA alert and the issue alive in the community with statements such as "The shame is that everyone knows where our poor are."[4] The result is more maneuverability for policymakers on issues that directly or indirectly affect these categories of persons than might be expected if the subject of being black or being poor were openly debated. In later chapters many of those cover issues will arise, including alleged violence in village centers, the sliding scale of payment, maintenance complaints about lower income housing, teen problems, community center programming, and funding for programs with few black participants.

The sub rosa handling of problems concerning race and class is also an important power resource for enterprising politicians. The political career of one of the major actors in the case studies in later chapters was strengthened by his position on before and after school day-care programs operated by CA in the elementary schools. His covert negotiations resulted in a strong recommendation from CA staff to the executive committee that after school care be provided free of charge, a startling change in policy. This suggests that CA's uneasiness about the neglected or unresponsive sectors of the population can be relatively easily tapped by and for these neglected categories of people if done out of the public eye. It also points out that the CA staff understands the constraints that the ideology of heterogeneity imposes on citizens, often forcing them to accept a fait accompli when a decision reaches the public arena.

Political collectivism among blacks is at an informal and rudimentary stage. Race is nearly unmentionable at public and even most private meetings, indicating a much heavier constraint on discussing "the black problem" than on discussing "the lower income problem." Elected black representatives in the community (at that time, two out of 35) are extremely cautious about identifying an issue as touching on race. The black candidates who have run for village board office have won easily, often with the highest number of votes, and have consistently but covertly protected the interests of black residents. However, the race of these board members is almost never acknowledged by them or by others.

When the members of an alternative life-style collective asked for permission to address one village board about racial antagonisms and violence, the chairman reported publicly that he had denied their request on the ground that it came too late for inclusion on the agenda. Privately, he told me he was extremely apprehensive about the reactions of the black members of his board on this issue, "I often find myself losing items to do with race at the bottom of agendas to avoid the hostility that invariably arises," he said. I have witnessed this hostility and have observed that it is by no means one-sided and hardly ever explicit.

There is a great deal of concern among CA staff about what the black community wants. Why do issues about race never surface publicly? Why do so few blacks run for office? This question will be discussed at length in Chapter 4.

WHO GOVERNS?

Governance is an issue of great concern in Columbia. Nearly every year citizens have gathered together to study problems about how the community is run. In 1971 a task force was convened to evaluate "some of the basic concepts underlying the plan of Columbia and how these concepts have carried forward and developed."[5] In 1972 the problem was defined as the roles of the constituent parts of the governance structure. Specifically, this study was to take "a new look at roles and relationship . . . this would include a total reappraisal by setting aside the old or existing structures . . . with the emphasis being on what Columbia might be or should be in terms of community participation and all other relationships."[6] In 1973-74 attention focused on the goals of the Columbia Association, redefining the objective during the almost two-year study process as seeking "not to deal with CA goals or objectives, but predominately with its policies."[7]

Large-scale and expensive attitude surveys have become routine, with attention given primarily to the satisfaction or dissatisfaction of residents, particularly in the area of governance. The perceived amount of influence in decision making is continually sought and reflects a deep-seated wariness within the Columbia Association about citizens' reactions to its administrative decision making and a concurrent uneasiness among the citizenry that the Columbia Association is not responsive. That only 16 percent of those most recently surveyed felt they had no influence on the process,[8] or that the Columbia Association frenetically seeks to facilitate citizen involvement in its policymaking, does little to stem the tide of this uneasiness. There remains a pervasive concern that the governance structure is needlessly complicated, unwieldy, and unresponsive, that the relationship between its constituent parts is unclear, and that the low level of community participation reflects these inadequacies and signals failure of the system.

The planners envisioned Columbia as a participatory democracy where individuals would be guaranteed access to the decision-making structures of the community. In this ideal system citizens were not only guaranteed access, but it was also assumed they would accept this mandate and regularly turn out in large numbers to exercise their rights. The idea that citizen participation is at the heart of the system has been widely promulgated. This probably reflects the planners' intuitive understanding of the problems inherent in translating authority into power.

This problem faces all political systems; it is particularly critical in Columbia where, except in the case of the legally enforceable protective covenants,* the quasi-governmental structure of the Columbia Association faces the continual problem of the legitimation of its authority. This problem can be seen in the concern on the part of both CA and citizens about identifying goals for resident participation and developing a plan of action to achieve optimum citizen participation. The following kinds of statements are typical of many elicited when residents are questioned about the administrative and elective structure:

> There has been a disappointing lack of interest. People don't come out to the public meetings.

> We need a lot of community involvement so that people can get together and express new ideas.

> If enough people get interested, things will be done.

> We need to strengthen the local organization at grassroots level in order to maintain the original goals of Columbia.

> The Columbia Association is developing into a bureaucracy and doesn't keep in touch with the people.[9]

These statements show that the amount of citizen participation has become the symbol for effectiveness of the system of governance. That is to say, citizen participation, through the planners' initial vision and through continual elaboration since then, has become the standard myth about how the quasi-governmental authority of the Columbia Association is legitimated. On the one hand, there is a continued uneasiness that low levels of participation signal the failure of the system to function in a healthy way. On the other hand, there is substantial evidence that the Columbia Association is a viable institution that, against great odds in terms of the intricacies of legitimation of authority inherent in its quasi-governmental structure, is extremely effective in meeting the needs and goals of the city's residents while at the same time seeking to assure its financial soundness. To put it another way, the power of Columbia's formal decision-making bodies is questioned by both residents and public officials because the legitimacy of broad public participation is absent, and yet a closer

---

*These covenants have yet to be legally tested and thus do not constitute a significant variation in the problem of translating authority into power.

examination indicates a rather effective political mechanism. Is there indeed a disjunction between the formal system of authority and informal sources of power? How in fact do the visible political units maneuver in a situation of low public participation for the legitimacy they need to transform authority into power?

The persons holding the five elected positions on the village association boards of directors in each of Columbia's five villages constitute one source of power in the community. One often hears variations on the phrase, "Village boards have no power." This idea about powerlessness is reinforced when only a small fraction of Columbia's residents participate in local elections, and when Wilde Lake, with its history of early and fruitful citizen involvement in the political process, has a difficult time finding candidates in village elections. CA is visibly concerned about this state of affairs. This tension may be a critical sign that, although village boards at times constitute a serious challenge to CA's legitimacy, they are needed as an important source of legitimacy. CA faces a double-bind situation in its relationship with village boards. If the idea is allowed to fester and grow in the community that village boards have no power, CA will lose in the process an important source of legitimacy. The situation is not simple, however; an "uppity" village board that is successfully drawing legitimacy from its constituency can be a tremendous drain on the energies of CA staff as they seek to harness this board for their own purposes.

The Harper's Choice village board (1973-74) is a good case in point. During this period Harper's Choice kept CA staff on edge during the entire budget process.* Because this board had withdrawn from the Columbia Combined Boards (as the name implies, a body made up to negotiate joint concerns of all village boards) over procedural and policy issues, CA was forced to duplicate its presentation and public hearing efforts by meeting separately at each stage with Harper's Choice alone. This was an interesting and difficult process to monitor. Besides the numerous public meetings that took place, many closed sessions with heads of departments within CA were

---

*The most important public decisions CA must make each year concern how it will spend its money. The budget process, a lengthy and grueling effort to legitimate these decisions in the community, begins in September with village level hearings and ends in March when CA's board of directors listens to CA staff's recommendations and makes the final allocation decisions.

scheduled, and individual board members of Harper's Choice carried on countless private lobbying efforts by dropping in at the CA offices on a daily basis. What transpired, in short, was a laborious but good-natured compromise that maximized the interests of both CA and Harper's Choice. In the final public budget sessions, Harper's Choice emerged as CA's most powerful source of strength.

CA staff was "worn into the ground" by this two-pronged effort and remained mystified about their "success" with Harper's Choice. My opinion was often sought: "Why is Harper's Choice so reasonable?" "Why can't the other village boards be like them?" "Why is this particular village board so good to work with?" I spent countless hours pondering this question with the firm belief that the explanation must have more to do with power relationships than with individual members' political expertise or personalities. Contrary to other village boards, Harper's Choice had experienced little turnover in the previous elections and thus had well-developed ways of working together. The most important of these followed a consensus model where, although members held widely divergent views on basic issues and disagreement was often far from friendly, debate continued almost interminably until agreement was reached. This process was witnessed often enough by members of the community and the press to engender a sense of the meaningfulness of the political actions of this board and fostered support that legitimized the actions of the board. Moreover, the adversary role they adopted vis-a-vis the other village boards was taken very seriously by Harper's Choice and explained to the public (usually by letters to or interviews with the press) in a similarly serious manner. This seriousness on the part of Harper's Choice resulted in support from the community and respect from CA. People in Columbia have difficulty defining the political relationships, but they know and covet effective power when they see it.

CA, however, continued to view the problems of governance as lying with the lack of citizen participation, with the added twist that communication between village boards and CA was faulty (in contrast to the good communication that existed between CA and Harper's Choice). They hastened to take the following two actions immediately at the close of the budget process. First, they hired a consultant to prepare a written document describing the relationship between village boards and CA for the purpose of briefing new village board members about the "reality of the system." The resulting report indicates that CA missed the implications of its successful confrontation with Harper's Choice. This document reads in part:

> Columbia's Village Associations have exactly the same power that any other civic association has: the power (and it can be considerable) of an active, concerned citizenry. Although they work together and consult each other on numerous issues and projects, the Village Associations and the Columbia Association are entirely independent of each other. As independent organizations, they influence each other, yet neither has control of the other.[10]

In this statement CA is still cherishing the notion that an active citizenry is the key to the system. The emphasis on the independence of the Columbia Association and the village associations reflects CA's concern about rumors that surfaced during and after the budget process that CA and Harper's Choice were in collusion. The importance of an adversary process between CA and the village boards is implicitly denied in the consultant's discussion.

CA's second action was to finance a weekend communications conference. The invitees included CA policymaking staff members and elected community representatives. Most planned to attend with enthusiasm. A consultant in intergroup relations was hired to "facilitate communication" at the conference and to "sound out the community" for a few days beforehand. This is added evidence that CA was still constrained by the fear of confrontation and conflict between itself and the village boards, and by a fear that "politics do not belong in a situation where the needs and interests of residents are the major concern of both associations." In fact, open confrontation as adversaries in the process of compromise seeking, both between CA and village boards and between village boards and their constituencies, engenders a sense of legitimacy in village boards that countless hearings on resident needs and desires do not provide.

The council reps are another category of elected officials. Perhaps the greatest difference between this category and village boards is that council reps have a great deal more status than power. These representatives are inhibited by the dominance of HRD appointees on the executive committee. The confusion between the alternative models of adversary and advocacy relationship between village boards and CA further threatens the position of council representatives as the residents' voice on the executive committee.

The result is that council reps have few effective mechanisms through which to seek legitimacy. On the rare occasions when they join forces with each other and oppose the HRD appointees on the executive committee, they are usually defeated. This means that they do not often risk exhibiting the discrepancy between their status and their power, and thus take few controversial public positions. Because of the prevailing myth of their importance, largely a product of the fact that they are, after all, the forerunners of the time when Columbians will be governing themselves, they serve mostly as legitimators of CA's decisions with the residents. For CA this is important; for the council reps and their constituency it often approaches being a sham.

Advisory bodies play an interesting set of roles in the legitimation process and, as with council reps, often reflect the confusions in the relationship between village boards and CA. Thirty-one such resident advisory committees are listed in a briefing book prepared by CA, and their interests range from biking to teen councils to early childhood education.[11] The latter is one of the most active of these bodies and reflects the strong commitment of Columbia's planners and early residents not only to the development of the community's children, but also to improving the quality of life for women. That this body is extremely active is a commentary on the controversial nature of community-supported early childhood education, particularly day care. Significant segments of the community, although not openly opposed to the concept, surface in opposition when their money is at stake, and questions about the detrimental effects of day care and the appropriate role of mothers are argued loudly. On the other hand, this area constitutes the only truly innovative social program in which CA was involved at the time. The efforts to maintain this involvement throw into relief some of the ways CA attempts to gain legitimacy.

Advisory committee members are appointed by village boards, two by each board, usually chosen because of expertise in the field. As experts, these advisors face difficulties between their role as experts and that of "providing an effective mechanism for broad-based resident participation."[12] Broad-based resident interest most often focuses on financing problems, while the advisors have actually been chosen for their potential input to program soundness. The conflict is that great programs often cost too much money. This is a serious problem; even more serious, though, is the double-bind situation advisory committee members find themselves in as mediators between CA and village boards.

One village board chairman discussed this problem at length. He said "the two appointees of the board are called upon to make decisions under time pressures that do not allow village consideration." (I have found this to occur, reflecting CA's manipulation of the advisory committee toward leading rather than reflecting village board views.) He reported that when he approached the advisory committee members for information on what CA would propose for early childhood education in the budget process, the appointee "became extremely protective, saying that I would be getting my copy of the proposal soon." He went on to say: "It became perfectly obvious that she was afraid that the information she had might be used by the board to argue against the CA position. I gathered from this that they have been told not to tell the boards what is going on." In closing he mentioned being "seriously uncomfortable with the expansion of the CA advisory committee system."

These advisory bodies were designed to be advocates for the needs and interests of the residents of their villages or for their village boards, who would presumably have already sought the opinions of village residents. In effect, the system works in the opposite direction. Advisory committees are indeed advocates, but of CA's position to village boards. The difficulties inherent in this position reflect the discrepancy between how the system actually works and the ideal; moreover, it attests to the empirical situation of CA and village boards as adversaries. Advisory committees have assumed this role precisely because the mythology about the cooperative CA-village board relationship is not in line with the political reality.

An added dimension of advisory committee importance to CA was touched upon briefly before. Columbia is a community of experts on every conceivable subject. The advisory committee system allows CA to thwart potential criticism from citizens who are experts by providing them with a vested interest in the system. This is another case where residents, usually without understanding the full implications, exchange potential power as concerned residents for status as advisory committee members, and thereby hand over their power to CA.

Although the newsstands carry other papers that include substantial coverage of Columbia news, the *Columbia Flier*, a free weekly delivered to every doorstep, constitutes the most important local news source to residents. This may be the most important source of legitimacy available to the Columbia Association *and* to the village boards. When asked what newspapers are read regularly, 92 percent of the respondents in the Neighborhood Evaluation Survey carried out in spring 1973 listed the *Columbia Flier*. This wide readership is important for it suggests a considerable spread of shared knowledge within the community. What is critical to this examination of authority and power sources, however, is the role of the *Columbia Flier* in the political process. The local news reporter for this weekly (later editor and general manager) is a potent source of power for the key actors of the political scene as they maneuver with each other. Some of the arenas of competition that arise in Columbia have already been identified. Some of the issues that serve as sources of legitimacy, as conveyed in articles and editorials in the *Columbia Flier* during the period of research, will now be examined.

In a June 20, 1973 article entitled "The People Tree Is Not the Statue of Liberty,"* the following discussion of Columbia's socioeconomic diversity appears:

> Where are our poor, our tired, our old? . . . Where are our "blue collar" workers, those 2,700 men and women who work at General Electric? . . . Where are the 6,500 construction workers who are building this city? They are not here. Not in Columbia where more than one out of four residents has completed post-graduate work. . . . We're such a success we can't even miss the middle income resident, the senior citizen on a pension. . . . If Jim Rouse can have the vision to create a city with as much going for it as Columbia, why can't his team of experts . . . come up with a way to meet their original goal? . . . Why shouldn't CA—that highly-rated unprecedented public corporation with all its borrowing power and potential wealth—step in to save the city from becoming a ghetto of upper middle class people? . . . Do we want future new cities to be built only for that portion of the population that is already well-taken care of in affluent America?

The idea that CA should address itself to the growing homogeneity in the community did not originate with this editorial. CA

---

*The "people tree" is the logo of Columbia and appears in many places around the community and on Columbia Association letterheads.

had considered making a financial commitment to additional low-income housing in private, informal discussions for some weeks preceding the article. What is important is that the idea was transmitted to the community in this fashion, and that shortly thereafter a formal but private discussion of the subject between CA staff and interested elected officials took place. At this session several versions of what CA might be able to contribute were hammered into a proposal to be presented to the CA executive committee by one of the council reps. In public session the executive committee voted to establish a contingency fund of $10,000 to study the possible contributions CA might make to increase the low- to moderate-income housing in Columbia.

The role of the press in this case was critical in at least two ways. First, by presenting the idea to the public that Columbia was failing to live up to its social goals, the consciousness of the community was raised and the opportunity for disagreement to surface was offered. Second, CA was publicly notified of strong support if it were to concern itself with the issue. The *Columbia Flier* was in the position of being willing and able to offer legitimacy for CA's involvement in this controversial area. In fact, it was clear CA would risk further public criticism in the newspaper if it failed to consider the possible roles it could play.

In a commentary on June 27, 1973 titled "CA Breakthrough: Take from the Rich, Take from the Poor," strong criticism is again leveled at CA:

> If you listen to CA's good intentions with only one ear, Columbia's quasi-government would warm the hearts of Florence Nightingale, Henry Thoreau and Saul Alinsky. . . . Just this week, for example, they present a petting zoo, an incipient country club and, so they tell us, help for the masses who can't afford to swim in our neighborhood pools. . . . Next we learn CA wants to spend $285,073 for the city's first urban renewal project—in Hobbit's Glen. [Hobbit's Glen is one of the high prestige, single-family home neighborhoods in Columbia.] Apparently the golf course clubhouse was depreciating the property values in the neighborhood.
> . . . Shocked at the idea that the mere combination of a restaurant, lounge, expanded pro shop, swimming pool, golf course, brand new rest rooms and maybe an eventual tennis court or two could be likened to an exclusive country club, CA prefers to speak of an "inclusive country club" . . . if some are willing to pay more, then CA is willing to take more—in order to help all those other

"poor" people. Kind of like Robin Hood. . . . What can we look forward to in the months ahead? CA will certainly continue to get mileage out of Earn-a-Membership, sliding scale day care, extra swimming pools, programmed activities for youth, friendly security guards at the lake. They have to keep us happy with something until the biggest breakthrough of all—a sliding scale, Earn-a-Membership admission to the country club's first charity ball. Set-ups gratis, of course.

Following the appearance of this commentary residents turned out in large numbers to oppose the idea of a private country club as antithetical to the concept of Columbia. The idea died a swift death (in fact, CA denied having such a plan in the same issue, indicating the intricacies of the communication flow between CA and the press), and nothing has been heard of it in this form since. Renovation of the clubhouse has been approved although not to the extent that CA proposed; this approval was given with the understanding that plans did not include eventual incorporation as a private club. In this case the community was successfully mobilized by the press on the basis of the ideology of equal access to facilities and services. CA tested an idea and lost.

In the following commentary of October 25, 1973, the *Columbia Flier* focused attention on the village board's recommendations to CA staff:

CA President Padraic Kennedy has repeatedly noted, "the key to CA is whether it will be property-oriented or people-oriented." The village boards' suggested priorities lean heavily on the property side. . . . As usual, each village wants better land maintenance and more trees, paths and play area. . . . Human services, that arm of CA dedicated to identifying and developing "the means to meet human needs of Columbia residents that are not currently being met by CA or other institutions" is given short shrift. . . . Why . . . do village boards—and apparently an apathetic citizenry—allow this division to be mired in conflict over whether we should subsidize programs for young children, to be reduced to viewing recreation as sports activities and to relegate community services to welcome coffees and socials? . . . What about legal aid, job counseling services, leadership training, housing needs, educational scholarships? And what about women? No mention of women by any of the village boards. . . . Thus far, the village boards have done little more than reflect a suburban concept of Columbia.

This article notified the village boards that they would have to be more innovative and direct more attention to social concerns if they were to have access to the power that approval of the press can offer. Job placement, housing needs, counseling, and women's needs surfaced as issues in the community in short order, and support for programs in many of these areas was obtained from CA.

It is always difficult to pinpoint the direction of the causal chain between press reports and policymaking. There is evidence that in some instances CA initiates issues with the press; more often, reporters, stimulated by a few key individuals around town to venture into unexplored territory, are the initiators. Regardless, what occurs is an action-and-reaction chain where CA makes use of the power of the press to consolidate its own power.

This brief analysis of the relationship among authority, legitimacy, and power provides a necessary background for understanding the formal and informal roles that will be played by the actors (both individual and corporate) in the detailed case studies that follow. Before leaving this subject, however, it should be noted that in the 1974 elections several Columbia residents moved solidly into the Howard County political structure, which created an immediate ambience of political cohesiveness within the Columbia community. The hardening of Columbia's political boundaries with the realization of its political clout in a larger social system has resulted in a political awareness in the community that will no doubt affect the configuration of power alignments within Columbia. All political structures are segmentary in that categories of individuals switch alliances depending on circumstance. There are possible ramifications that this increased demarcation between Columbia and the county may have for the generation of new and different sets of political interactions within the community. For example, it is conceivable that the apolitical character of Columbia's decision-making mechanisms in terms of national political party alliances or divisions based on liberal and conservative dichotomies of national significance will change, and that intervillage competition will be reduced or take new forms as Columbia coalesces as a city with political power in relation to the county. Further, it might be predicted that the reality of being a political entity with battles to fight vis-a-vis the county and the state will encourage more overt political collectivism around issues such as race, class, and women's rights within Columbia.

NOTES

1	Columbia Association 1974b
2	Columbia Association 1974b
3	Columbia Association 1973
4	*Columbia Flyer*, June 20, 1973
5	Columbia Association 1972b
6	Columbia Association 1972b
7	Columbia Association 1974a
8	Columbia Association 1973
9	Hollander 1972
10	Columbia Association 1974b
11	Columbia Association 1974b
12	Columbia Association 1974b

3

PRIVATE
PRIVILEGE VERSUS
PUBLIC RIGHTS

Ideas about rights in property are deeply entrenched in American ideology. These ideas are so well disseminated and reinforced that the discrepancy between the importance given to property ownership and property values and the belief in equality of opportunity for all persons is fairly well tolerated. To some extent this discrepancy is tolerated because most Americans share the goal of owning their own home. In Columbia, concepts about property and territoriality are safe and well-understood covers in controversies that actually concern the differential distribution of rank and privilege. As portrayed in the cases that follow, concepts about personal rights in property and public rights in open space provide the backdrop or medium individuals can employ to argue publicly about the system of rights and privileges that accompanies the accumulation of wealth in our society.

WHERE DO YOU LIVE?

Who lives where and in what kind of housing is a familiar topic of conversation in most communities. The language that is used in these conversations serves two related but rather different purposes. First, it communicates empirical facts; certain housing complexes are only available as rental units, for example. Second, and much more important, it facilitates communication of further, less acceptable (for open discussion, that is) information about presumed social differences between categories of people.

This process will be illustrated with an incident I recorded during a public meeting. At a Harper's Choice village board meeting in September 1973, a number of residents from the neighborhood of Longfellow were present to confront an attorney for the developer of a tract directly north of Eliot's Oak Road, the major thoroughfare in the neighborhood of Longfellow. Adjacent neighbors on Eliot's Oak Road and two affected cul-de-sacs questioned the premises of a rezoning petition for a higher density.

The attorney began by stating that 15 acres of the property would be developed in apartments and the remaining 31 acres in single-family homes. Under heavy questioning he admitted that the zoning for which he was applying would allow these single-family homes to be developed in semidetached housing instead. He hastily sought to allay the obvious anxieties of the audience with statements about the relatively high cost of these semidetached units (otherwise known as townhouses) and their small size. At one point he said these units would appeal very much to the young professional couple— implying, among other things, that there would be few children.

He went on to say the apartments would be in the section of land that did not adjoin Columbia residents' properties, while the single-family homes would be in the 31 acres closer to Longfellow. Moreover, he offered a 50-foot buffer between his development and the rear property lines on adjacent Longfellow property—at the cost of the developer. In answer to further questioning from the audience, he responded reluctantly that the apartments would be rental rather than condominium units. The residents began by complaining vigorously about the possible ill effects on the ecology of the area, particularly tree removal. In short order thereafter the concerns began to be worded in terms of property values. There was a great deal of uneasiness expressed about the lack of details available, and the residents were promised a special meeting with the developer that would include written information with drawings setting forth the specifics of the higher density plan.

In numerous settings where such a confrontation between builder and resident is played out, I have observed that ideas about protecting the ecology of the area, the difficulties of access in terms of present traffic patterns and volume, the proximity of the proposed housing to housing already in existence, and the stress on existing facilities (most often mentioned is the elementary school in the neighborhood) are continually debated in the early stages of the discussion. If the builder or his representative is not sufficiently conciliatory, and does not make it clear that the proposed housing is intended, for example, "for small families of substantial means," the residents will often move to statements such as "this kind of housing does not belong in this kind of neighborhood." Builders have become very adept at manipulating the private language of prestige. Note, for example, that in the above case the representative tried to avoid raising anxiety in the audience through use of the phrase single-family home as a misleading cover for the fact that these would be townhouses, or semidetached housing. Moreover, he was careful to avoid the loaded term multifamily by using the phrase semidetached. In the most successful of these confrontations (successful for the builder, that is), builders exhibit an understanding of the unspoken questions about what kinds of people will buy their houses and manipulate the widely shared understandings of what price range and style attract what kinds of people. With this form of cooperation, which allows information about certain other less controversial categories to be freely communicated, issues surrounding class can remain covert.

Owners and renters are two such relevant categories in Columbia. Following a planning rationale that people who rent are less likely to have cars than people who own their own homes, rental housing, while scattered in all villages and in most neighborhoods, is largely clustered around shopping facilities. Prestige neighborhoods such as Hobbit's Glen and The Birches do not include rental units, although in some highly desirable neighborhoods such as Bryant Woods, rental units are well integrated with both owned townhouses and single-family detached homes.

Although village names seem to carry very little categorization, there is a general awareness that the west side of Columbia is more heterogeneous socioeconomically, by age, and in the number of single people. This neighborhood is also considered by many to be more desirable, and thus it is more expensive to live here (much as it is lately quite fashionable for families to return to the center city). In the early days of Columbia rental units were given four, and owned units five digit street numbers, and the west side still largely follows this pattern. In general, however, even without this informal information-conveying device, people tend to know a great deal about what type of housing is where. With a simple question about the neighborhood and street name, an individual can be categorized by housing type, ownership or rental status, and price range (although definitely not by race).

There are abundant indications that property ownership is a sorting device of some importance. As one respondent said in answer to a question about his expectations of the community, "We are homeowners now and that gives us a sense of belonging to the community."[1] Homeownership carries with it an informal set of obligations that range from caring more about the looks of where one lives to being concerned and running for office. Evidently these obligations confer a set of unspoken rights, for public participation in decision-making structures is largely limited to property owners. This is, of course, contrary to the ideology, and people express dismay that apartment dwellers, often referred to as "renters," do not integrate themselves into the community.

Discussion about the protection of property values is a legitimate and convenient ritual often used to disguise other concerns. Its legitimacy is probably based on the fact that while open dichotomizing of owners and renters, with special attention to the rights of owners, neglects almost 40 percent of the city's population who do not own their own property, it is assumed that owners and renters alike are interested in the prestige of Columbia as a place to live, and thus, by implication, in property values. However, precisely because the concern for property values subsumes a number of other less acceptable concerns, much of the public decision-making debate centers on this issue in one way or another; an example of this can be seen in the Discovery Park episode later in this chapter. Because of the role that these concepts about property ownership serve in covering for more threatening concerns, there is an inordinate amount of attention given to property values in public debate. The result is that renters tend to find entering the political process uninteresting and unrewarding.

Dichotomizing single-family home and multifamily dwelling can be seen as an effort to communicate about social differences in situations where the terms own and rent are too value laden. There are some startling inconsistencies in the use of these concepts that are often overlooked in the process. For example, multifamily, used as it frequently is to convey lack of ownership rather than type of dwelling unit, is misleading; a large number of the multifamily dwellings in Columbia are townhouses and most of them are owner occupied. There is also an increasing number of condominium apartments that belong in the ownership category. Furthermore, because Columbia was designed and advertised as a "real city," and because of the consequent efforts to make better use of the land by increasing the density of dwelling units rather than surrounding each family with its own plot of green, there are prestigious townhouse clusters in Columbia as well as areas of prestigious single-family homes. Unless one says single-family detached, the label single-family might easily apply to townhouses or even to apartments. Yet more than one townhouse resident has told me that when asked over the telephone, "Is that a single-family home?" he or she feels constrained to reply, "No, a townhouse," or risk "putting on airs."

Multifamily units in Columbia include federally subsidized rental apartments and townhouses (approximately 500 units at present); moderately priced rental apartments (which house people of substantial resources as well as 60 percent of Columbia's under $8,000 a year population); luxury apartments and townhouses for rent; and owner-occupied condominium apartments and townhouses of both moderate and substantial price. Thus the term multifamily dwelling is sufficiently imprecise to allow individuals the flexibility of attaching the meaning they wish to the term and of using or not using it in order to convey ideas about status. For example, multifamily is never the term of choice when referring to the complex of luxury lakefront rental units called The Cove; instead it is termed lakefront luxury apartments or simply The Cove. The contradictions and ambiguities are tolerated, and are in fact useful, because they permit communication about the social differences viewed as inherent in most situations of owning and renting without disruption to the ideal scheme of equality.

Underlying this scheme is a system of beliefs that is rather widely held but rarely explicit: single family means property owner, multifamily means renter; renter implies the lack of resources to buy a home, and a lack of resources implies lower income. (There is an understanding, however, that young couples who rent or buy modest townhouses have a limited choice only temporarily, and are actually on the apartment to townhouse to single-family home ladder of prestige.) Further, to foreshadow the discussion in the chapters on race and class, lower income implies black, and both lower income and black imply more children, more noise, and less attention to property maintenance. These beliefs are pervasive, but can nevertheless be covered up or manipulated by selective use of the term multifamily; conversely, however, these beliefs must be carefully overcome when use of the term in a truly descriptive sense cannot be avoided (as in presentations before planning and zoning boards). In these cases the petition to build multifamily dwellings is quickly followed with statements such as "These will be luxury units beginning at $50,000," or "These will be very small units for the childless couple or small family."

What happens when categorizing on the basis of single family and multifamily is precluded, as in a case where all participants in a social scene are residents of owned multifamily dwellings? One such case is the cluster of 88 moderately priced, privately owned townhouses known as Bryant Square. Multifamily cannot be effective as a sorting device in this instance even though some of the units were purchased for investment and are occupied by renters. Although membership in the townhouse association is, by charter, open only to those who own a unit in the development, those who rent units are fully integrated into the social life of the development. Nevertheless, in early meetings of the townhouse association individuals felt free to categorize in terms of owners and renters. For example, it has been said that "we must contract for lawn maintenance for both association owned and privately owned areas as renters will not keep up their property."

This kind of statement was prevalent only during the first year that this cluster was occupied. There is evidence that the own/rent dichotomy was used less often in subsequent years as mobility increased the number of rentals and decreased the amount of information a resident could pass on that would identify the renters.* It may be that at this point in the developmental process of a neighborhood, the informal sorting out of owners and renters is too likely to cause offense if done openly. When this happens, the political aspects of the sorting process can be submerged (but not, I emphasize, lost) in the rhetoric of personal taste in friends that renders abstraction of the order in the system extremely difficult. That is to say, it is

---

*The mobility rate in Columbia is 40 percent annually, but higher in townhouses as people move up to a house and often retain the townhouse for investment.

unacceptable to fail to associate with one's neighbors because they are renters, but it is quite acceptable to keep one's distance because "we have nothing in common." This study has not investigated the categorical sorting that goes on in the private domain, such as friendships, neighborhood relationships, and the like. This is a rich and relatively untapped source of data on how people categorize others, particularly among middle-class Americans.

Immediately adjacent to Bryant Square is Roslyn Rise, one of the five clusters of the federally subsidized townhouse and apartment complex known as Interfaith Housing. One might expect the residents of Bryant Square to categorize residents of Roslyn Rise as renters (although certainly not as multifamily because both developments fit that description). They do not do so, possibly because there are a few renters among the Bryant Square residents as well. There seem to be no constraints in this situation on following quite openly the process implying that lower income means black, which in turn means noisy, too many children, and poor maintenance. Although these subsidized units are less than 40 percent black, people think they are 80 or 90 percent black and often refer to "large numbers of unruly children" (actually 1.3 per family in Bryant Square and 1.5 in Roslyn Rise) and to the prevalence and effects of "ghetto values." In fact, very few of the families in Roslyn Rise came from inner-city areas because priority was given to rural Howard County residents. It seems that simply because these units are federally subsidized and fairly isolated both socially and politically, at least in people's minds, the constraints placed by the Columbia ideology on socioeconomic and racial stereotyping are reduced. More will be said of this in the extended case study concerning Interfaith Housing in Chapter 6.

INSIDERS AND OUTSIDERS

Concepts about rights in and control of land also figure prominently in the process of sorting out who belongs where in the community. It may be recalled that along with racial and class heterogeneity, one of the features emphasized in the planning of Columbia was innovative land use. Thus, at the same time that 20 percent of the 15,000 acres was set aside as permanent open space, an effort was made to increase housing density as much as possible in favor of shared space (such as commonly held green areas in the midst of a townhouse cluster).

The original plans for Columbia incorporated a minibus system that has never materialized,* and the rights-of-way that were established for this system are now open to what has been referred to as "squatter's rights." This does not imply that people can build a house on this property. Rather, the first residents in the area may plant gardens in the space while newcomers may wish to play ball there. Usually it only becomes a contended resource if there are other overriding but unmentionable problems to do with class or race at stake.

As in most communities there are areas seen as public space. These include roads, shopping centers, and office building complexes, as well as parking spaces surrounding these. Public space, whether legally public or public in terms of its usage (such as shopping malls that are actually privately owned), means that one must expect to share that space with anyone else who may wish to be there.

Open space, that winding system of greenery, pathways, and lakes that is one of Columbia's major assets, is subtly but clearly a different matter. Although people expect to share the system of open space with people from outside the community "who don't contribute to its maintenance" (much as residents of any city think of their parks as public), some important differences emerge between public space and open space. There is often concern expressed about a large influx of "those people from Baltimore and Washington" fishing or picnicking in the open space around Wilde Lake, and a flurry one night when a rumor was passed that "outsiders" were camping out at the lake. In the process of investigating this rumor I was able to document what I suspected to be the case: "those people from Baltimore and Washington" and "outsiders" mean blacks, and beyond this, blacks who are not "our blacks."

Some areas that are part of the open space system are considered public at certain times. For example, the summer lakefront evening performances transform the open space of Lake Kittamaqundi and its surroundings into public space, with the mixed reactions of pride at being able to draw so many different people to Columbia, and

---

*Columbia did at this time operate an extensive public transportation system that was quite successful in terms of meeting many people's needs but less so financially.

dismay the "trouble caused by outsiders." Further, there are conno-
tations of "private" about open space that borders on one's private
property. Almost everyone wants the small play areas known in
Columbia as tot-lots, but almost no one wants a tot-lot in the open
space near one's own property. We will see in the Discovery Park
episode that the residents near that piece of wooded property held
very strong and opposing views about the appropriate use of open
space.

Public and private control of property are concepts of some
import among residents, although there are constraints inherent in
the Columbia concept on open discussion of the intersection of these
two categories of territoriality. There is a shared understanding that
the public control manifest in the architectural review system safe-
guards the right to an aesthetically pleasing environment for all
residents. However, problems arise when this value conflicts with the
ideology that says a man's home is his castle. In other words, the
advantage of having the attractiveness of the view from one's own
home protected by restrictive covenants is sometimes overlooked
when the right to paint one's front door purple is in question.

Columbia was planned to overcome what were seen as the ills
of urban environments. Public control in terms of legally enforceable
protective covenants, adjudicated and enforced by an architectural
review system, was intended to correct these ills. The review system
was accepted by every resident and business that bought or leased
property in the new town. There is evidence that this form of public
control was a significant point in the immediate marketing success of
the developer; in fact, it appears that individuals interpreted the
system as an important force in protecting their private interests
and minimized in their minds the aspect of public control.

The head of the Columbia Association's physical planning
division has stated that the covenants are intended to "keep property
values up and make Columbia a decent place to live, insuring that
one person doesn't ruin things for the rest of us." Perhaps the relatively effortless success in selling property that imposed restrictions
of these kinds on the purchasers was related to uneasiness in people's
minds about what would ensue in a community that was to be
balanced in terms of employment, land usage, income, and race.
Further, as will become clear in the confrontation between the
Wilde Lake architectural committee and the Interfaith Housing
Corporation, the threat of covenant enforcement and the concomitant

issues of public and individual interests have come to be used in power redistribution struggles as covers for other issues.

Earlier in this chapter we saw that concepts about the appropriate development of land often emerge in this sort of mystification process. Builders planning multifamily usage of land purchased from the developer must face the county planning and zoning authorities for approval, and often for revision of their plans even if approved. As Columbia's residents become increasingly aware of the political realities in the system, it has become commonplace for these builders to meet with the village board of the village in which the project is to be built to discuss the details of their plans. Village board meetings are regular (twice monthly) and public, and the inclusion of such an item on the agenda is publicized in advance. The process has evolved quite simply because residents, if they oppose the development in question, can and do garner their forces to oppose the plans at the county level. Thus, with a demeanor of respect for the rights of residents in the development area to have input into what will be built near them, and with compromises in hand in order to counter the fears of these residents, builders attempt to coopt this opposition before it enters the formally political domain.

The two case studies that follow illustrate the use of the categorical distinctions and symbolic language discussed above. It is important to recall the previously stated goal of the research as these cases are read: namely, to establish connections between categories of residents (for example, blacks, lower income, owners, renters) and the symbols (or hidden language) that allow the negotiations for power between these categories to remain largely covert.

TARZAN AND THE SPACE TROLLEY: CASE ONE

A meeting of the Wilde Lake village board in September 1973 marked the first public appearance of an issue that was to be contended for some weeks. Two opposing contingents of residents appeared before the board to discuss Discovery Park, an assortment of play equipment located in a heavily wooded area of Columbia Association open space near the homes of both groups (see Figure 3.1). The park was described as a "nuisance" by a small but irate group of residents (A), and a "uniquely attractive and successful" play area by a larger and equally vocal group (B). The park included two particularly

FIGURE 3.1: **Tarzan and the Space Trolley**

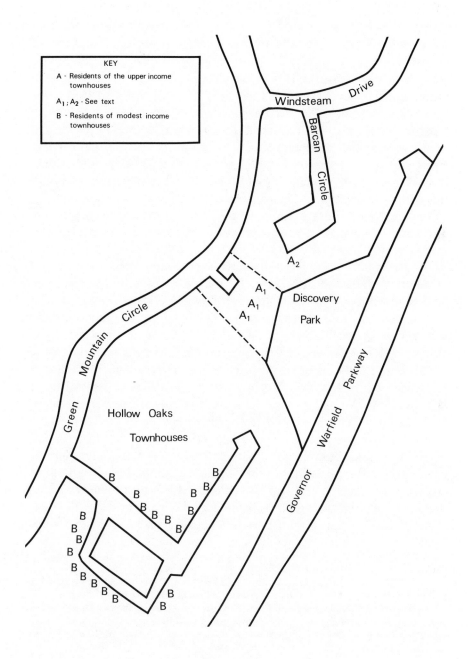

popular pieces of equipment, both attached to tall oak trees by a resident arborist. One of these is referred to as a Tarzan rope swing and the other as a space trolley. Each provides a swooping ride across the entire naturalistic and wooded area on equipment that almost everyone agrees fits in the setting in terms of design and material.

The discussion at this meeting raged on for two hours, with four families vigorously protesting the "noise, invasion, and destruction of our property."* Presenting the case of these four was Barry Landsman. He argued that he and his neighbors were not opposed to a play area in this particular area of open space, but to "two particularly attractive pieces of equipment that draw children older than those for which the facility was intended." He went on to say that the Tarzan swing and the space trolley "cause congestion and yelling, and make the area unsafe for young children." Further, he complained of "trash and damage to residents' property by these teenagers who shouldn't be using the facility."

The play area was designed and the equipment chosen by members of the Discovery Park committee, all of whom live in more modest townhouses referred to as Hollow Oaks (B). They protested at this meeting that it was "insane logic" to remove such popular equipment, proposing instead that similar play areas be constructed at other locations to disperse the large numbers of youngsters attracted to this area. "What is being objected to is the success of the facility," said a member of the committee. "It is the only successful playground in Columbia. Are we to give this up in the interests of perfect peace for four families?" She went on to chide Landsman: "I am shocked that a man of your stature should argue this way." Another resident of Hollow Oaks pointed out that the residents of this high density cluster of townhouses have had "plenty of noise in the streets of Hollow Oaks for the last four years, as well as noise from traffic on the four lane parkway directly behind this development." Furthermore, he said, "the developer didn't plan for proper play space for

---

*Three of these families (A₁ on the diagram) live in an attached set of luxurious homes in the wooded area directly adjacent to the equipment, and two of the household heads in these three families are employees of the developer and members of the Columbia Association board of directors. The fourth protester (A₂) lives in the end unit of a set of townhouses quite like those of the Hollow Oaks residents (B). The names of these individuals have been changed.

this kind of high density development or for access to this piece of open space."

Parenthetically, Landsman had been a chief planner for the developer since early in the project, adding an ironic twist to the Hollow Oaks's residents' complaint about the lack of sufficient play space and the proximity to the highway. Moreover, well before the initiation of this research, the Hollow Oaks residents had launched a successful attack, including sit-ins, on the builder of their development, charging that he was felling many more trees than necessary. Their ire was directed at the developer as well, and may be a significant historical factor in the development of the political consciousness evidenced by the Hollow Oaks's residents in this case.

A Wilde Lake board member urged a compromise solution, pointing out that this area "is common land owned by everyone on Columbia." Unexpectedly, Landsman proposed a compromise that would adjust the equipment to make it less attractive to older children and move it further into the woods. This proposal, while unanimously accepted with obvious relief by the board, seemed unacceptable to most of the Hollow Oaks residents and to the two opposing residents who were not Columbia Association officials. Nevertheless, a further resolution was passed by the board requesting CA to identify other sites for similar equipment and to improve the access to the site so that children would not continue to enter through the property of the four opposing families.

In October this controversy flared again because, as Hollow Oaks' residents put it, "in an overnight action the trolley has been unilaterally removed by CA." From the discussion at this public meeting it was possible to piece together what had occurred. George Abbey (A_2), one of the opposing residents who was not a CA official, had threatened CA with a lawsuit. He based his charge on the fact that before purchasing his property he had approached CA to establish the eventual use of the open space behind the house he proposed to purchase. He reported that at the time he was told "it will be a natural play area." It was clear that the present use did not, for him, constitute a natural use.

The president of the Columbia Association was present as a spectator at the rear of the meeting room, and spoke up about this potential lawsuit: "This statement about how the space would be used now represents gross misrepresentation on our part. When Mr. Abbey called and said he was instituting suit because he was tired of waiting, we removed the trolley." He went on to say that "there is a great need to clarify what is an appropriate use for open space and what procedures will balance majority and minority concerns."

One resident of Hollow Oaks remarked angrily, "There are two questions involved here: one is the removal of the trolley by CA, and the other is the use of open space generally. There is a persistent assumption that open space belongs to the people next to it. This is a question of the brutal use of power." Another resident of Hollow Oaks, who was also the designer of the Tarzan swing, said, "An agreement has been twice made and twice broken. There are only four opponents in this case, four *individuals*."

Landsman remarked, "There has always been a reciprocal use of this property, but this use is not consistent with the property I bought. Now it is a question, not of infringement of my property, but of my person." Beach, a resident of the prestigious townhouses along with Landsman, and general manager for the developer as well as a member of the CA board of directors, remarked, "We are distressed at being the only residential area with this kind of equipment."

A member of the Hollow Oaks contingent replied, "This play area was copied from one at Copperstone Circle—is that not a residential area?"* Further, he said there were two things at stake: "First, the legal issue involves a misunderstanding of property rights, and second, there is the issue of change. This play area does not put people who live in these three houses in any different position than that of many people who live in townhouse communities. Many back up to parkways with high noise levels. The issue is that life changed for these people when they didn't expect it." Another resident, turning to address the CA president in the rear of the room, said, "By CA's unilateral removal we now have a mini-Watergate. . . . The residents feel that there are two things: Mr. Abbey's suit and the fact that not everyone would have gotten this preferential treatment. There are 140 very angry families, and they deserve an apology."

The Wilde Lake village board supported the Hollow Oaks residents fully during this meeting and conveyed to those CA staff members present their anger that "the rightful position of the board as arbitrators of the issue has been usurped." The result was

---

*There is sarcasm in this remark. Copperstone Circle is a federally subsidized (FHA 236) garden apartment development on the east side of Columbia.

that the CA staff members present at the meeting agreed to return the space trolley to the site and to install several others in locations around Columbia. Thus, they agreed to abide by the mutual CA and village board decision reached earlier.

This controversy was argued by the complainants as an issue of personal rights in property and countered by the designers and builders of the play area as an issue of public rights in commonly held land. Both sides are in fact discussing the differential distribution of rights and privileges. The resolution in favor of the Hollow Oaks residents reflects the concepts of personal rights in property and public rights in open space as simply the backdrop or medium that people could use to argue publicly about the system of rights and privileges that accompanies the accumulation of wealth and prestige in our society.*

There is indeed a significant difference in the prestige of these two housing clusters. This is reflected in their relative monetary value; the three prestigious units were at the time of the research each valued at between $75,000 and $100,000, while the units in Hollow Oaks were between $35,000 and $50,000 (although considerably less expensive for first purchasers). The elegance of the three-townhouse unit mitigates against its being subsumed under the category of either townhouse or multifamily. This is illustrated by one resident's statement during the conflict: "The people who live in these three houses are not in any different position than the many people who live in townhouse communities." Despite intensive efforts in the planning of Columbia to redefine the larger society's evaluation of single-family dwellings as most desirable, "townhouse" still has a connotation of a housing choice that reflects financial limitations.† Quite clearly the owners of these three prestigious units are not limited in choice; thus the units are referred to as houses rather than townhouses.

Further, we can see that Landman's statement, "this use is not consistent with the property I bought," comes very close to

---

*The stress any family would undergo if suddenly a large group of youngsters, not their own, appeared on a regular basis "at all hours of the day and night" on property they had come to regard as an extension of their own is not denied here. The families defending the equipment, however, felt that in this case some people's stress was regarded as more important than their own.

†To extend this point, one of the most active builders in Columbia markets his townhouse units as "townhomes," an effort, it would seem, to add prestige.

open acknowledgment that development of commonly held land should depend on the value of the personal property on which it borders. This is a more revealing statement than is usually made in public, the kind that sometimes emerges when the stakes are high and the disagreement marked by accelerating public argument.

Early in this dispute, before flaring tempers removed some of the constraints, differential privilege could be hidden under egalitarian statements about the rights that normally accrue to the owners of property. Because a convenient route of access to the play area was through the private property of the higher priced townhouse owners, there was indeed "invasion and destruction of . . . property." However, additions to this statement the next time it was uttered point out that the issue is not simple. When Landsman complained of the "trash and damage to residents' property by these teenagers who shouldn't be using the facility," he implied that trash and damage caused by children who should be using the facility would be acceptable, or that more appropriate children would not leave trash or cause damage.

This foreshadows a discussion that will appear in the next chapter: categorization by age (teenagers) is often a cover for a host of other less acceptable stereotypes. When people argue for the exclusion of "older children" from play facilities, they in effect try to limit its use to children in the immediate neighborhood and, therefore, as mini-neighborhood homogeneity is often the case, to the children of, for example, middle-class, upwardly mobile families. When Landsman argued that "it is a question, not of infringement of my *property*, but of my *person*," he again removed the cover that property rights and property values offers, and exposed personal privilege as the contested resource.

The constraints on acknowledging this issue as reflective of the coincidence of wealth and privilege are evident in the statements of the defenders of the play area as well. The question "Are we to give up in the interests of perfect peace for four families?" leaves unspoken the issue of social difference between the power and prestige of the four families and that of the Hollow Oaks residents. Indeed, there seemed to be an immense amount of restraint in the room on both occasions. Although angry rambling among contacts in the village outside of formal, public sessions was heard,* the most open state-

---

*For example, "Rich people control a lot more than the land they own," and "Landsman and Beach can write their own ticket in Columbia."

ments of these residents' concern that they were being treated in an unequal and unfair fashion mentioned the "noise we have had to tolerate" because of the large numbers of children in high density living, the idea that "open space belongs to the people next to it," and this action as "a brutal use of power." However, most of these resentments about unequal treatment were hidden in statements such as, "the issue is that life changed for these people when they didn't expect it."

Landsman's capitulation toward the end of the first meeting may have reflected his sudden awareness that everyone in the room understood the issue as one of differential privilege while not openly saying so. His offer of a compromise followed closely the comment that it was shocking "for a man of Mr. Landsman's stature to argue this way." It was a measure of the extreme stress this "invasion of privacy" was causing Landsman that he allowed himself to be put in this unattractive public posture and to return for more criticism on the second occasion. No doubt the situation was sufficiently intolerable that he and Beach were willing to risk a public test of their power. Nevertheless, it is surprising that these individuals could have hoped for a resolution in their favor given the ideology of Columbia.

DOGS, GRASS, AND FENCES: CASE TWO

In March, 1974 the Merion Station Townhouse Association, representing a large group of owners of traditional, moderately priced townhouses in the village of Harper's Choice, submitted an exterior alteration application to the Harper's Choice Resident Architectural Committee.* These residents asked "to erect a three rail rustic fence . . . to extend approximately 310 feet on the east boundary line between Merion Station and Tilbury Woods Apartments." (Tilbury Woods, while not federally subsidized, housed largely lower income renters.) The application gave the following reasons supporting the approval of the fence:

> 1) to prevent dogs from entering premises; 2) to prevent trespassing over lawns (used for shortcuts); 3) to prevent parking in front of

---

*A full description of the architectural review system that is operative in Columbia appears in Chapter 6.

homes by residents of Tilbury Woods; 4) to prevent delivery trucks
making deliveries to Tilbury Woods from driving over grounds; 5)
to reduce and deter potential for continued vandalism and theft.

The application for a fence was denied by the Resident Architectural Committee in a written communication that made no
comment on the reasons for the denial. This action raised the ire of
the Merion Station residents, and at their request a public meeting
was planned among the residents of Merion Station, the chairman of
the architectural committee, and the Harper's Choice village board.
The chairman of the architectural committee, a black man, resisted
the pressures of the residents of Merion Station during this meeting
to recommend a change in the decision. He pointed out that, "the
committee considered this application very carefully, and felt that
there was more that wasn't said than was." He went on to say that
the concept of Columbia was to leave the open space alone, and
"that the spirit of this new town was what you didn't address in your
application." He continued in a tentative manner: "I apologize if
this isn't so, but the committee felt that maybe there is a tendency
to set this group apart, to ostracize this area [Tilbury Woods] by
totally fencing it off."

The two representatives of the Merion Station residents then
spoke up. One expressed resentment "at your questioning of our
motives," while the other said "we *know* where these problems are
coming from, and the residents, the *homeowners*, feel this fence will
help." The one black member of the Harper's Choice village board
interjected a comment about considering the "psychological impact
of this fence" on the residents of Tilbury Woods. It was suggested
by another board member that the erection of a fence that would be
attractive would surely fail to deter pedestrian traffic or dogs, and
that "the exclusionary impression such a fence would give might
actually increase vandalism." Although discussion about types of
fencing or plantings that might be acceptable continued for some
time, the decision of the architectural committee was not reversed.

Fences are generally considered inimical to the ideology and
aesthetics of Columbia. Although limited privacy screening to protect
a family's activities from public view is allowed, architectural committee approval of the plans must be sought, and it is incumbent on the
applicant to provide an attractive fence (usually with plantings as
well) that considers the rights of neighbors to a pleasing view. Fencing

to limit access to an area is discouraged as contrary to the image, both psychological and physical, of Columbia as a "garden for people."

Tilbury Woods Apartments are moderately priced rental units, and represent the best housing bargain in Columbia for those who do not qualify for subsidized housing; a large number of the city's lower income population live here. The apartments have a generally negative image. For example, I was present when a black graduate student applied at the main office in downtown Columbia that handles all rental properties. He was warned: "You wouldn't be comfortable with the kind of people who live there." Even though it is widely expressed that "Tilbury isn't a good place to live," the criticisms are usually not stated in terms of the people who live there but in terms of issues like poor maintenance.

The wording of the fence application in this case indicates the care that is taken to avoid categorizing people negatively and to reword issues to express concern with, for example, invasion of dogs, damage to lawns, and infringement on personal parking privileges. The open mention of vandalism in the application is unusual, and was kept carefully in line at the public meeting. Vandalism was treated as an incidental issue in the long and serious discussion of what kind of fencing would protect the Merion Station residents' grass and plantings from dogs and from people "taking short-cuts"; theft, although mentioned in the application, was never brought up. Nevertheless, everyone in the room seemed aware that these residents were trying to protect themselves from a different kind of people. Because this is contrary to the ideology of Columbia, the issue had to be talked about in a way that would communicate concern with these differences, while at the same time protecting the image of an open and egalitarian community.

It is impossible to be certain that the racial mixture in the room during the discussion of this case affected what was said and not said; however, never before had I witnessed the *public* questioning of a group of residents' motives as contrary to the ideals of Columbia. There was a great deal of uncomfortableness on the part of the black architectural committee chairman and an almost excruciating tentativeness in his statements about the exclusionary purpose of the fence. The one black member of the Harper's Choice village board did not speak up to support the chairman for awhile; it appeared that he waited to see what his white fellow board members would or would not say before committing himself. I am left with the impression that the presence of black actors in this case was important, and discuss this issue at some length in the next chapter.

PRIVATE PRIVILEGE VERSUS PUBLIC RIGHTS

The foregoing disputes are important for three reasons. First, they provide examples of how property rights can cover for issues that are inimical to the normative order that denies rank and privilege. Second, they provide tools for abstracting some of the symbolic strategies individuals use to increase the amount of control they have over their social space, be it defined as private property, open space, neighborhood, or whatever. Third, the dispositions of the complaints (that is, replacement of the trolley and continued denial of the fence application) serve as illustrations of the strength of the Columbia ideology of equal access, particularly in combination with the ethic of participatory democracy, which makes it more difficult for this sort of issue to be settled in private negotiation.

There are widely held assumptions about the association between class rank and residence in rental housing and multifamily housing. When the empirical situation obviously contradicts these assumptions (as in the three luxury townhouses in the Discovery Park case), the symbolic markers that imply class are conveniently dropped. Aside from these situations, however, there is general acceptance of an articulating chain of assumptions: residence in rental housing implies the lack of resources to buy a home, and a lack of resources implies lower income; lower income implies more children, more noise, and less attention to property maintenance, and thus less desirable neighbors. Through the American ideology that places high value on owning one's own home, these symbols have attained a general enough acceptance to allow for widespread use as a device for categorical sorting that is relatively uncontroversial.

I have attempted to illustrate some of the ways people deal with the lack of fit between the ideal set of beliefs and values they hold in the back of their heads and the facts of social interaction and stratification on the ground. Recalling an earlier discussion, the normative order of Columbians is made up of two major components: first, there is the ideal scheme of community that characterizes American society in general, and second, there is the ideology of Columbia as the "Next America," carefully designed to draw residents on the basis of these ideals about community. Underlying the pragmatic adaptation of Americans to the exigencies of living and getting ahead in a democratic, free enterprise system is a deeply felt belief in equality of opportunity for all persons. The concept of community envisions the mutually supportive relationships of individuals pursuing a good life without constraint of previous family or individual attainment, as well as the opportunity to participate freely in the decision-making process. This ideology has always held that it takes many different kinds of people to make a community, while at the same time falling short of indicating just why this might be so. These ideas were picked up in the planning and publicity for this new town. Columbia was to provide, first and foremost, economic diversity that would cut across cultural, religious, and racial lines. "To foster human growth" was a major goal. Variously and frequently mentioned in this regard were the creation of "a complete and balanced community," preventative health maintenance within the economic grasp of all who lived in the community, ecumenical religious facilities, housing integrated both racially and socioeconomically, and a decision-making structure that emphasized community participation at all levels.[2]

These ideas embody what is known as the "Columbia concept." A random sample of citizens, questioned in 1972 about their reasons for moving to the community, identified this concept in some of the following ways.[3]

You have an opportunity to grow with the community and help shape it. Citizens have a voice in the government.

We liked the concept, the idea of being able to identify with a small community.

There is a sense of community, a feeling people have for each other. You know your neighbor and feel something about the community.

We liked the idea of Columbia's being open in terms of racial and economic groupings. People aren't concentrated in economic and racial groups.

I agreed with the concept of Columbia, that is, the people wanting to take part in the government.

The way Columbia is set up makes it easy for everyone who lives here to have a say in how it is run.

> Everyone is new here. We all need help and are all striving for the same goal.

> Columbia needs people to be involved so it's encouraging to feel needed and wanted.

> The way it's set up helps the smaller people have a voice.

It is evident that people are primarily concerned with feeling a part of something larger than themselves and their families, and that this manifests itself in expressing a desire to have a say in how things are done. (Public participation in governing appeared as an issue in the discussion of concepts of authority and legitimacy in Chapter 2.) The fact that few Columbians exercise their right to participate in the decision-making process is reminiscent of patterns in the larger society, and points to the relevance of these kinds of ideas as value statements about equal access to decision making. They represent, in other words, negative evaluations of differential privilege rather than a desire for large-scale public participation in daily decision making.

There was a careful attempt to establish Columbia without special privilege accruing to the property owner.* Rights in all community land, services, and facilities, as well as the obligation to contribute to their operation and maintenance, were assured through automatic membership in the Columbia Association. While only property owners directly pay the annual assessment, individuals and families in rental housing in the community contribute their share through the rent structure. This reflects the intention in the design of the Columbia Association to assure that all residents (whether property owners or not) would both contribute to the costs of providing these services and benefit through use of them and through equal access to the decision-making structures.

Even with this goal firmly in mind, however, there was an early hint of dichotomizing property owners and the rest of the community. For example, in material given to all residents when they move to Columbia, the village associations are described to be "formed exclusively for the preservation of the good and welfare of the residents and property-owners of the village." Several examples of conflict over the distribution of resources in Columbia have indicated how this concept of property can serve as a cover for other,

---

*Reston, Virginia, on the other hand, is "governed" by a home owner's association.

more volatile, concerns already discussed, such as racial separation and antagonism, class isolation, and lack of access to decision-making structures.

We have been concerned with two sorts of information that seem in conflict with each other. On the one hand, there is the system of beliefs, the ideology, about what the community should be like. On the other hand, the empirical evidence from nonpublic occasions and conversations indicates that the reality is far different from the ideal. The case studies presented draw from the rhetoric of public confrontation to begin to illustrate how a system of communication exists that allows people to deal with this lack of fit without openly confronting it and to reaffirm, in a sense, the Columbia concept of a balanced community by refusing to participate in the use of ideas, such as trespassing and the nuisance of dogs, as covers for exclusionary actions.

The following chapters will further develop this argument. They will show the relationship between the system of communication about rights and obligations and the ways that the privileged hold power and the less privileged challenge their ability, if not their right, to do so.

NOTES

1   Hollander 1972
2   Columbia Association 1972b
3   Hollander 1972

4

BLACKS AND WHITES

RACISM HAS GONE UNDERGROUND: CASE THREE

In summer 1973 an organization called Peer, an all-white political and social collective whose message was aimed mainly at black and white young adults in Columbia and the rest of Howard County, sent a letter to influential county residents and officials soliciting their opinion about the racial problems they said (citing considerable evidence) existed in Columbia. The letter asked for further information in preparation for the third issue of their newspaper, *Changes*, and said that this upcoming issue would discuss black-white conflicts in Columbia, the oppression of blacks, and racism. In particular, the group asked for comments on the "recent incidents in Columbia of attacks on and terrorizing of white teens by a group of black men, teenage and older." The letter went on to point out that this "violence feeds the racism of white teens and their parents," and asked for input from "the community."

The Howard County Police Department responded to a reporter from the *Columbia Times* and was quoted in an article in that countywide newspaper on August 9, 1973. The police department spokesman stated that "the letter did not point out anything new to us," and noted that "assaults by groups of youth move in and out of various areas of Columbia. Trouble at Wilde Center has died down, for example, but incidents at Oakland Mills Center increased several months ago."

Members of the collective requested permission to meet with village boards to receive their reactions to the letter. I was present on the evening when the group met separately with both the Wilde Lake and the Harper's Choice boards. There was an air of tension and hostility at the meeting with Wilde Lake; particularly charged were the interchanges between the collective members and one black member of the board.* She appeared resentful at both the charges about black attacks on white youths and the "presumptuousness that *you* might suggest what would be good for black youth in Columbia."† The three white members of the board quietly tried to smooth things over; one acknowledged, for example, "I am beginning to have to accept that there are racial problems in Columbia." Nevertheless, the atmosphere was still charged with the resentment of both black board members when the Peer group left to make their presentation at Harper's Choice.

At the Harper's Choice meeting the ambience was quite different. Each board member was introduced to the members of the collective, who returned the courtesy. One board member said, "there is indeed racism in homes, good single-family homes,†† both black and white." Another pointed out that "when people move to an open community they think of themselves as liberal while racist tendencies linger on. What you're doing in the sense of making it public is a large first step. Only a small portion of the problem is violence; this just scrapes the surface. Racism has gone underground in Columbia."

Several weeks later the collective distributed a flyer in the Wilde Lake High School following a series of racially motivated confrontations in the school; it included, on one side of the single sheet,

---

*At this point in the late summer and fall of 1973, there were for a short time two black women on the Wilde Lake village board.

†The Peer letter had suggested, and the group amplified on the point at the meeting, that "there is only one model for blacks in Columbia—sports," and suggested that funding should be made available for arts.

††Note that this board member is employing the symbolic dichotomy single-family home (and by implication, multifamily dwelling) discussed previously to express that middle-class people of this status are also racist.

"A Message to Black Students," and on the other, "A Message to White Students." To blacks the group pointed out that the anger black students feel toward white students should be directed at the "adult white community [who] use the police and the prison to get rid of you," and suggested that white racist society is the enemy of both black and white students. The message to the white students pointed out that "blacks are beating us up because they aren't strong enough to beat up their real enemies." Further, "if we depend on the police or the school system to protect us, instead of learning to protect ourselves, we will be helping these systems continue to victimize blacks."

By the time I was informed of the distribution at the school and hurried to the scene, faculty had confiscated the flyer from most students, and not a single copy was in evidence. School had just been regularly dismissed, and a departing white student overheard my inquiries about where I could obtain a copy and offered his, remarking with derision, "You can have this one; I'm certainly not interested in it."

Shortly after this flyer was distributed, I had a lengthy, informal chat with a black woman, manager of one of the five Interfaith sites and parent of one of the youths who were suspended after "beatings" at Wilde Lake High School. She and her husband are sophisticated about race relations and are middle class in orientation. She said she had talked to the black assistant principal twice in the past week and had expressed her disagreement with allowing these incidents to be termed racial. He told her there was "no getting around this fact." She expressed a great deal of concern about the safety of her son. Her next-door neighbor's son, also part of the group suspended, had been badly beaten by "three white brothers from a Hobbit's Glen family"* who were reported to have vowed to beat up "each black kid who was on the principal's list." Yet she went on to say that "parts of the Peer flyer offended me, and all of it is inflammatory and trouble-making." "After all, there is violence in all high schools," she said, a statement I hear over and over in Columbia, from both blacks and whites.

We went on to talk about life for blacks in Columbia. She said "blacks have always counted for nothing, and that isn't going to change.

---

*Hobbit's Glen is Columbia's most affluent neighborhood.

Just tell me how blacks have any more power here than in Baltimore."
When I hinted that black kids might feel freer to "throw down the
stairs" (a common phrase at Wilde Lake High) any white kid who
called him nigger, a great deal of her restraint vanished. She mentioned
a series of seemingly unrelated issues: there had been a distinct
improvement in the attitude of Howard County police toward blacks
since Columbia became part of the county, the Howard County
NAACP was getting press coverage for the first time, a "black person
can demand courtesy everywhere in Columbia," and a black clerk
can feel free to be rude to a white customer.

It became clear that violence was serving a myriad of functions
in Columbia. Empirically, it is at the very least a disconcerting fact;
to many people it is highly disturbing. The task of this chapter
is to sort out the symbolic uses of the terms. The concluding chapter
will discuss how the empirical patterns of violence are changing and
speculate on what this may mean about power reorganization and
patterns of social change in this community.

There are two tendencies evident in the above case. First,
violence among young adults is "nothing new," and only when flare-
ups reach the public arena, which they rarely do, will a wide range of
people discuss it openly. For example, only when an incident is
under investigation will the police freely discuss the "assaults by
groups of youth." Thus, there is a strong tendency to hide the verbal
and physical hassling that goes on by denying its existence between
incidents of public disclosure. Second, when there is unavoidable
public discussion of violent episodes, an effort is made to relate it
to anything but racial animosity. Middle-class blacks exert a great
deal of control over the discussion of violence in Columbia. Numerous
interviews with blacks after documented racial skirmishes brought
consistent and vehement denial of racial motivations. The black
principal, although he would like to, cannot deny race as an issue
because he is too close to it every day; the black mother simply
cannot cope with the idea that her son might physically harm a white
youth "just because he is white."* With an all-white audience, the
all-white village board can more openly discuss racism and violence;
the village board that is racially mixed is plagued with hostility

---

*It should be made clear that the more liberal members of the community (black
and white) worked hard to document white instigation of violent episodes (such as taunts,
epithets) with some success.

whenever these issues arise and the chairman finds himself "losing items at the bottom of the agenda when they touch on race." The fact that this research was conducted by a white investigator of course leaves open the question of what the symbolism would be, or if it would disappear, in conversations within all-black groups.

Do blacks have something to gain in maintaining this cover? What do blacks say about race in Columbia? In casual conversation with blacks who developed some trust about my work, I discovered a widespread resentment that "Columbia, the Columbia Association, and whites in general are unwilling to accept the idea that there is a black community." It is said that tremendous financial support is available for swimming, for example, which is a "white sport," while repeated attempts for financing of a strong boxing program have met with failure. The saga of the teen centers is often recalled; when the second teen center became all black, teen centers were decentralized so that each one had a specialty such as the arts, sports, and the like, and well-loved black personnel were fired or reassigned. This shuffling turned out to be a "complete failure," say some blacks, and removed a successful program for black teens. Several blacks have expressed anger at having their blackness treated as "an interesting frill," mentioning as examples Black History Week or two- and three-day black arts festivals that fail to be approved for program support on a more permanent basis. There is explicit anger about the complaints about black youth who allegedly harass people in village centers. This has been referred to by blacks as the "paranoia whites suffer whenever more than two black youths speak above a whisper."

Whites, on the other hand, talk of potential violence, and these murmurings are usually overtly or covertly associated with race. One well-respected white teacher reports requesting and receiving a transfer from a highly regarded elementary school because of racial tensions. She says that hostile and angry black parents are instilling racism in their children. She has known many of these parents for several years, and they did not hate whites previously. The principal of this school, a popular and effective man by reputation, has been transferred and replaced by a black man. A white village board member mentioned that reverse discrimination exists at Wilde Lake High School. She reports that whites exhibiting boisterous behavior in the media center, for example, are subject to disciplinary action, while "blacks are not even reprimanded."

Nevertheless, Columbia's greatest success lies in the racial integration of its housing. Columbians are extremely proud of this success; it is probably the largest single contributor to the idea of Columbia as the "Next America." The problems that are seen to be associated with race, then, are subject to two, largely unconscious, strategies: first, these problems are often magnified because they are such a threat to people's image of what the community is supposed to be; and second, a complicated set of symbolic categories is devised as a cover-up for the perceived failures. The second of these is where our interest focuses, for this mystification process permits people to mediate the lack of fit between the set of values and beliefs that guide their lives and the situation in which they in fact live.

TEENS AS A SYMBOL

One hears and reads frequently about teens in Columbia. Teens is empirically a misnomer; members of the reference group for this categorization range in age from thirteen to the mid-twenties. In general it is used quite loosely to refer to anyone who might qualify for or use a teen program and anyone who might exhibit behavior associated with teens, such as hanging around village centers or the lakefront. Two common references will display quite different referents in the use of the word, and will indicate some of the complexities of the mystification process. When people say, "What shall we do about the problem with teens?" they tend to mean black teens, or black young adults of high school age and older, who congregate in public places. They also refer to the pervasive separation between black and white teens. On the other hand, when people say, "What else can be done for teens?" they tend to mean white or at least middle-class teens representing the age category usually associated with the word teenage (thirteen through high school graduation), and to refer to the fact that unstructured programming other than athletics has rarely been successful in drawing this group.

Usually the "teen problem" refers to a widely known but seldom discussed fact in Columbia: young adults socially segregate themselves by race. Because young adults are subject to forced congregation daily in school, this is much more obvious than social patterns of adult society are likely to be. Adult Columbians murmur continually about this separateness and the corresponding "failure of teen centers" to draw both black and white young adults.

The following description of the progression of a series of youth behaviors in regard to teen centers, and the corresponding reactions of adult Columbians, illustrates the group boundaries that are evident under certain circumstances. Blacks and whites, as well as youths and adults, sometimes say that things were a lot better when the unstructured teen center programs were operating and "the kids were allowed to sort themselves out as they wanted." These statements refer to the period extending from the opening of the first teen center until the early 1970s. For example, in 1971 and 1972 there were three centers (Wilde Lake, Harper's Choice, and Oakland Mills), each concentrating on supervised drop-in sessions and planned activities such as dances, jam sessions, and trips. During most of this time, the Wilde Lake center was largely attended by black youths while the other two centers drew mostly white participants. There was little or no resentment among young adults about this distribution at the time. While white young adults from Wilde Lake "had to go to Harper's Choice or Oakland Mills," and black young adults from these villages came to Wilde Lake, the separation by race was not total by any means. A young adult black woman was quoted in the press: "It's a myth about the teen center being all black; it's a lie that it was a black ghetto. White kids did go there."[1] Although adult Columbians worried about this racial separation, the concern did not turn into action until there were signs that both the other centers "were becoming black." In June 1973 the Columbia Association transferred teen responsibilities from the recreation department to the department of community services, and "many heads were put together to look for a solution to the teen problem."

In August 1973 the elected officers of the Harper's Choice teen center were asked to make a semiannual report to the village board. After several minutes of questions to which the four white officers of the teen center had no answers (for example, "I haven't been here all summer," and "I've been out of town"), board members became increasingly annoyed and pressed for answers. After whispering with several other teens one girl spoke out. She said she was sure the board was aware that since the present officers had been elected, use of the teen center had become limited to blacks. "There's nothing for us here, so we go to the pools and the lake." When questioned about why they stopped attending, another girl said that "just walking down the stairs into the center means being pinched and commented on by black males, and I don't like it." She said that not having a black band at a teen dance means that "no blacks come and vice versa." The teen center director (a white) spoke up from the back of the room to say that teen centers are always patronized by cliques, and that this is a clique problem, not a racial problem. The teen center officers exchanged looks of boredom and disbelief. A black resident, present for a later item on the agenda, said he resented the implication that behavior "common to all teens" (sexual comments) was taken to be an aberration when indulged in by blacks. The teen center officers warned that fights that "went on all the time around here in the spring" would begin again when the pools and the lake programs end in the fall. There was no response from board members except to thank the teens for coming, and they filed out.

This incident represents one of the rare occasions during 18 months of intensive fieldwork that I witnessed the public discussion of the racial separation of young adults. Moreover, it seemed clear on this occasion that if the board members had anticipated the direction the discussion would take, no one would have witnessed the above. The effectiveness of the constraints on discussing racial problems in public cannot be overemphasized. The above incident is important, as is the Peer collective incident, as an example of the unusual instance when the constraints were temporarily removed.

The plan to revamp the teen centers into "activity centers," with each reflecting a focus on, for example, performing arts or athletics, coincided with the firing of some well-loved part-time staff. This move, without input or advance notice to the teen center members, displeased many black and white teen center participants and some parents. This idea of theme-centered teen activities took shape and died in short order. By the end of January 1974, the teen center concept was virtually abandoned. In 1973 CA had poured a significant amount of money into teen center staffing and programming. This new plan to "integrate teens into community center life," entailing no center staff and a large dependence on user-pay, structured programming such as classes in karate, meant that this financial investment would be reduced in 1974 to 25 percent of the 1973 commitment. During this budget period, Oakland Mills board members and volunteers involved in the management of the community center successfully lobbied for $20,000 to operate an experimental teen program in their village center. The arguments for funding, although usually not worded this explicitly, concerned the urgency "not to abandon the effort to serve a socioeconomic and racial mix of young adults." The success they experienced in gaining funding in a fiscally conservative year is a measure of the power of this ideology when carefully and covertly manipulated.

At the time that the decision was made to scuttle teen drop-in activities entirely except at Oakland Mills, a very small fraction of Columbia's teen population was actually using the centers. Moreover, without enlightened and comradely supervision, the situation had turned out to be one of "vandalism, writing on walls, broken chairs, and a severe trash problem with half a dozen or more whiskey and wine bottles each night." The director of one of the community centers complained to me, "Harold [a black community services employee] wants me to let these guys eat the food they've stolen from the Giant in the kitchen while the village board members want me to shoot them on sight." Within two weeks after this statement was made, the teen center was closed.

REFLECTIONS IN ADULT SOCIETY

From the data gathered on occasions when adults discuss "the teen problem," some interesting categorizations emerge. Teens can mean white or black young adults or both; if there is a problem over and above mere lack of participation in programs, it usually means black teens. However, the symbolic category (teens) covers some further implicit categorizations. Black teens as a category is rarely heard because it is understood in certain of the usages of the word teens. If black teens is used, it generally does not refer to the young adults of Columbia's middle-class black professionals; rather, it implies lower income black teens, "those from the ghetto who haven't ever lived in a place like Columbia and have different values." "Everyone knows" that these young people have weak or absent fathers, working mothers, disrupted family structures, and generally unhealthy home environments. The process ramifies further: among these lower income teens there are those who are proper recipients of "our attention and our dollars" (the insiders, our own poor), and those who are not (the outsiders "who come from the county or from Baltimore and D.C."). Thus the model that people in the community have in their heads when they say teens looks like figure 4.1.

This model represents the conceptions of adult Columbians; it is not suggested as an empirical description of young adult society. In fact, young adults are locked into a power struggle that permits very little fragmentation among blacks or whites. White young adults say that blacks stick together and report that although "the black kid who gives a white kid trouble" is usually not in the main-

FIGURE 4.1: Reflections in Adult Society When Adults Discuss Young Adults

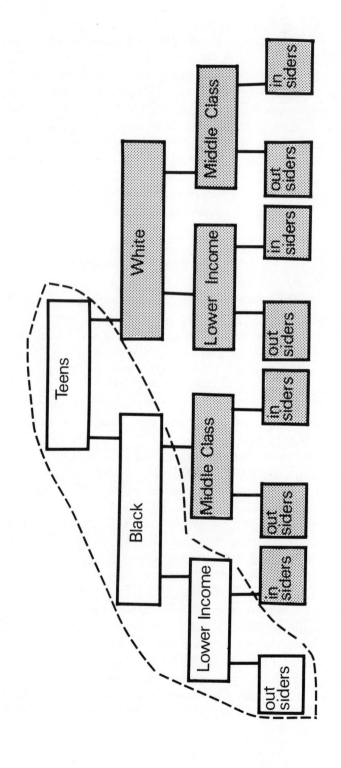

stream of the school either academically or in athletics, other blacks who are will linger on the fringe of the fracas offering moral support or watching complacently. Although the division between "freaks" and "jocks" so well-known in white high schools is present among whites, it is less pronounced here; a significant percentage of white teens are neither, and their existence as independents tends to mesh the two groups. Athletes (jocks if white) and white girls dating blacks are more able to float between black and white society. Occasions where young adults form a category facing adult society (football games or graduation activities) significantly reduce the boundaries between blacks and whites.

The saga of the teen centers is an example of CA staff's attempts to change what they saw as a racial, separatist trend among young adults into an integrated situation. One result was the fragmentation of black teens by class; middle-class youth retreated from the unattractively redesigned teen programs to their family club rooms, and lower income youth from inside and outside of Columbia remained at the unsupervised centers with nothing to do. So in a sense, not only do adults see young adults with the categorizations set forth in the above diagram, but at times they force the divisions to occur.

Although adults will talk, if less than comfortably, about these ideas and practices among young people, it is much more difficult to ferret out the categorizations as they are utilized to sort and re-sort adults and households. There is a startling similarity, however, between the model adults use when discussing teens and what emerges when one observes adults in conflicting situations. As in the case with young adults, white adults do relatively little categorization of themselves. Lower income whites, although somewhat more than 50 percent of the lower income population, does not seem to be a relevant category.* Adult middle-class Columbia will not verbally accept the suggestion that it is socially segregated by race as young adult Columbia will (or must because it is so obvious). This makes the first division in the young adult diagram one that is not accepted among adults as a model for Columbia in general and one that is extremely difficult to get informants to discuss. It seems, as the diagram below attempts to show, that the values of the middle class

---

*This, however, may have as much to do with the fact that a sizable proportion of lower income whites are students or middle-class families in temporary adversity as that whites choose not to fragment their power.

from the next division reach up and pull black and white adults together to maintain the image of an integrated community—so important, for one thing, to middle-class property values. Lower income becomes synonymous with lower income black, (ignoring the fact that roughly half of this population is white). This category is further divided into insiders and outsiders (the blacks who often fish in Wilde Lake are constantly discussed: "Are they from Columbia?" which is acceptable, or "Are they from Baltimore?" which causes anxiety). Thus the model adults have for teens can be viewed somewhat differently when considering the community as a whole. The point is that adults recognize this basic structure in terms of young adults and are perplexed and anxious about it; they do not recognize it as characteristic of the community at large.

CRIME

The concern with the teen problem has a counterpart that also often covers for the unmentionable category of race: a seeming persistent concern with the problem of crime. Crime can mean home and merchant burglaries or physical attacks with weapons, such as personal robbery or rape. There is a great deal of talk about locking and lighting, and Ryland Homes (a prominent builder in the area) cemented its reputation for community spirit by offering a service of home identification of personal possessions "to reduce crime." In Bryant Square, the cluster of townhouses that neighbors one of the sites of subsidized housing, there was an immediate flurry upon occupancy to install rear gates and double-locks on front doors, and the townhouse association pays an exorbitant electric bill to maintain an intense level of lighting, purportedly "to discourage vandalism." Empirically, crime in Columbia does not surpass that in other urbanized suburban communities in the area such as Silver Spring and Bethesda, Maryland. In Bryant Square I know of two burglaries in 18 months of occupancy, both of which involved young white adults who lived in the development. Moreover, a significant amount of Columbia's crime is assumed to be drug related; at least one active home burglary ring is said to be composed of white drop-outs supporting drug habits.

Nevertheless, the talk of crime is consistently associated with race in people's minds. There is less concern with personal safety and the loss of personal property than with the status of the communi-

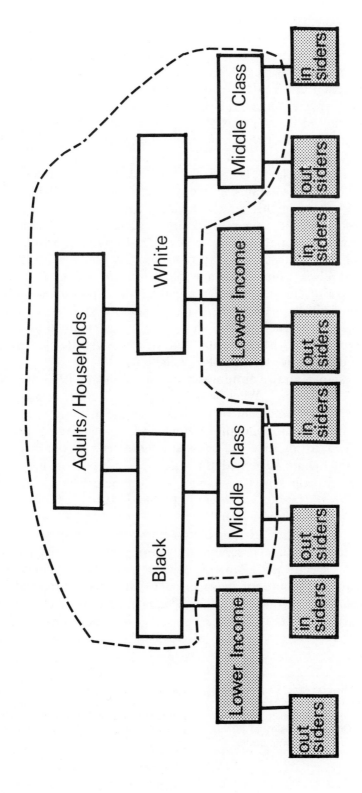

FIGURE 4.2: Reflections in Adult Society When Adults Discuss Themselves

ty ("Columbia was not supposed to be crime-ridden like Baltimore or Washington"; "We made the decision to move way out here to get away from crime and violence"), and thus the real fear seems to be about property values. It is said that crime only came to Columbia when subsidized housing was built, a recurrence with slight variation of the widespread belief that prejudice only came to Columbia when subsidized housing was built. This brings up the familiar connection between race and class. There is a chain of implication that associates crime with subsidized housing, and subsidized housing with blackness. The chain flows in this direction rather than centering on a more direct association between race and crime (such as persists in the larger society) because of the effort to deemphasize race, consistent with the ideology of the community (and also, no doubt, with the fact that most black Columbians are solidly middle class). People are quite aware of the dangers of ruminating about crime too often or too openly, both because of the damage such rumors will do to the image of the community, and because they tend to be sophisticated enough to anticipate that talk of crime will quickly turn to race and be offensive to their black neighbors.

Examples drawn from a survey carried out in 1973 may help to clarify the point. When asked about problems associated with teenagers, only 16 percent of the respondents felt these were fewer than in the previous community in which they had lived.* Further, when asked to identify the cause for more teen-related problems, 12 percent openly suggested that the racial mixture or presence of low-income people was to blame, and some responded with the category of outside teens. When respondents were questioned about whether they take casual walks at night, 44 percent responded in the never category, with 20 percent of these mentioning the lack of safety due to crime, and several others bringing up the insufficiency of lighting specifically. Moreover, when directly questioned about the adequacy of outdoor lighting for walking in the neighborhood, 36 percent replied that it was not adequate. Twenty-six percent of those surveyed felt their home was not safe enough from criminal

---

*Although only 22 percent replied that these problems were more than before, 32 percent found them to be about the same. Because expectations about the quality of life are known to be extremely high in new communities, answers that include ideas about satisfaction with this quality of life are likely, when they respond by saying no change, to reflect more concern with the issue than is indicated.

break-in, while only one percent of these suggested they were unsafe because of "undesirable people in the neighborhood."[2]

THE COVER ON RACE

Discussion of teen problems, inadequate lighting, crime, and lack of personal safety represents the use of safe concepts to communicate a concern with the threat of racial mixing that cannot be expressed openly because of the constraints of the ideology of a successfully integrated community. The worry about these issues is way out of proportion to any actual situations I have observed. For example, teen problems: there have been almost limitless jobs for young adults in Columbia, comfortable and abundant space in warm months to lie around, smoke grass, and drink with little harassment, and a 16-year driving age that makes the bowling alleys, restaurants, nightclubs, and rock concerts on the fringes of Baltimore and Washington accessible. Another example is the inadequacy of outdoor lighting. Columbia is very well lit at night. These statements are symbols, not realities, and it is understood well enough by the people who use them, although rarely acknowledged, that communication about race can occur in an orderly fashion without disrupting the ideal image of a racially mixed, peaceful, and cohesive community; that is, without directly referring to race.

It is possible that the hostility exhibited by black board members when issues of race are overtly discussed may represent a choice, perhaps unconscious, to control the discussion of race and thus to limit some kinds of interferences in their lives. By passing up the right to influence policy openly in terms of what blacks want, blacks also avoid the public obligation to be accountable for problems such as what can be done about gangs. It may be that blacks, from long experience, understand that the only time white society is interested in race is when the life of the community is not proceeding smoothly according to white, middle-class values. Given that this may indeed be the case, the pressure to participate would seem to far outweigh the rights and benefits that would accrue, and lack of public participation in the decision-making process by blacks then becomes more understandable. To put it another way, the benefits of identifying themselves as a black interest group are limited.

Under the present circumstances of a silent black minority, the rare occasion when the cover is removed always centers on problems.

No one ever asks "What do blacks want?" unless there are visible signs of alienation that intrude into the peaceful and cohesive image of the community. Since middle-class professional black adults are unlikely to be alienated enough to spoil the image (they have, after all, an active cultural and social organization and the financial resources to support it), the problems usually arise among young adults and lower income blacks. When they do, blacks and whites in general cooperate to explain away these failures as, in one way or another, beyond the community. In general this means that the troublemakers are outsiders, either from outside Columbia, or from outside the mainstream of Columbia. Thus, they are "in their early twenties but emotionally still teenagers," "from homes where there's no dinner and no family," "from the County, Washington, or Baltimore," or "from the ghetto." Moreover, statements like, "This problem has never been solved in any other community in the United States," absolves middle-class Columbia from responsibility, and the issue of race returns underground. The separatism and hostility in the high school are harder to explain away. It is clear that "kids from good, single-family homes" are involved, and the evidence that this is not a black problem but a black and white problem is hard to avoid. But then, prejudice has a pervasive and long-lasting life, people say.

That issues of class are more penetrable and lower income residents more accessible says less about the relevance of socio-economic status over race in the social and political workings of this community than might seem to be the case. If we take into account only the fact that young adults line up by race rather than by class, we can see that class is not more relevant than race in any simple way. Although middle-class blacks are largely invisible as a category in terms of cultural differentiation and political collectivism, there are signs, also evident in the larger society, that emphasis on blackness is becoming more prevalent. Moreover, the tendency of the few black elected officials to support positions that reflect a concern with the less-advantaged minority in Columbia (that is, issues to do with the sliding scale of payment, day care, violence, community center programming, and teen centers) is notable. I suggest that blacks of all classes have kept their cultural differentiation invisible for a reason, albeit an unconscious one. These differences are a source of power and can be used to manipulate the ideology of integration so important to the community. At the same time, however, coming up front as an interest group could make blacks vulnerable to cooptation by the dominant cultural group (whites) in the community. Signs appeared near the end of this research that this invisible stage might be coming to an end; for example, an advertisement in the local newspaper carried the following caption: "BLACK PEOPLE are a BIG people . . . A Strong People. We should stick together . . . become united." Whether or not a significant change comes about in the relative visibility of Columbia's black population, nothing could be further from the truth than the statement, "the problem in Columbia is one of class, not race."

The respect and assertiveness between black and white adults observed in public places suggests that the segregation of youth in the high school, who are after all members of the families of these same adults, must reflect something more than simply prejudice. Black and white youth in Columbia separate themselves from each other just as they do in other schools characterized by large-scale desegregation efforts. Yet many observers agree that the atmosphere, in the schools and elsewhere in Columbia, is different. Could not this separation in Columbia be a relatively harmless competition where cultural differences are the raw material with which to negotiate new rules about power? Different patterns of dress, different tastes in music and styles of dancing, and different interests mark the boundaries between black and white adolescent society. Although the form of these cultural markers that youth choose to display is much the same as in other biracial circumstances, the primary function of fostering these differences does not seem to be separation or racism. Blacks are not interested in less interaction but rather in equal choices—the only way to get there is to use the ideology of Columbia to take all the power that the ideology will force people to part with.

It has been difficult to find situations in the community outside the high school where an interface between some sort of black community and the visible decision-making structure or other white elites could be identified. (Adults do not ordinarily yell nigger and honkie at each other.) Although important, it is easy to overinterpret the fact that whether we looked at the persons who appeared around controversial issues, or at the symbols that recurrently appeared when people seemed to be talking about race, the language of class was invariably used to discuss the issue. This can prove misleading because underlying the controversies that are worded in terms of class, the notion of race continues to persist. That people think subsidized housing is almost all black, contrary to fact, indicates that being lower income is inextricably bound up with being black in the minds of whites. But the rhetoric of class has in most cases successfully subsumed or covered for race.

IS THERE A BLACK COMMUNITY?

More and more often, the question of whether there is a black community in Columbia arises. Both blacks and whites tend at times to confirm and at other times to deny the existence of such an entity. The black head of community services for the Columbia Association was asked in a press interview if he saw any way that the black community could help with the violent episodes between white and black youth at the lakefront. He replied:

> I'm not sure there is a black community here, and maybe that's part of the problem. There are a lot of black people, but no defined community. . . . The median income for blacks in Columbia is not much different from the median income for whites. Many blacks have paid the price to get here, so to speak, and really don't want to be reminded. And then there are some sincere, dedicated blacks who want to help but just don't know how. They say, "What can I do?" And there is no one to answer them.

A white village board member said, "Since I've come to Columbia I've noticed that there are no black community leaders here. Maybe that's because there is no black community." On the other hand, blacks have complained that "the white community refuses to accept that there is a black community in Columbia."

Whites may long for a black community to emerge when help is needed with recalcitrant black youth, or with a flagging teen program. The fear and disapproval expressed at the use of the black power motif during a lakefront talent show in the summer of 1974, however, indicates that a coalescing black consciousness crossing class boundaries and emphasizing cultural differentiation is most decidedly not what whites want. Of what are whites afraid? Blacks say whites worry that if Columbia becomes "a really good place for blacks to live," it will become a predominately black city. Some of these same blacks have mentioned that when they have children, or when their preschool children reach elementary school age, they will leave Columbia "because it is not a good place for blacks to raise children." Thinking that these informants meant racial animosities as the problem, I was surprised when they went on to discuss the difficulty of conveying to their children "the richness of a black cultural heritage in this middle-of-the-road place."

There indeed seems to be a sense of community among blacks, but as any sort of empirical entity it is elusive. There are the public manifestations that suggest some sort of social and political cohesiveness. Blacks were largely absent at most events I attended as part of my personal life. The subscription film series, the bluegrass evenings at the lakefront, the discotheque in downtown Columbia, a public lecture on China, the Women's Center, and most of the public decision-making gatherings such as budget hearings are largely attended by whites. On the other hand, large social gatherings of blacks who have rented the indoor swimming pool and a rock band for dances on weekends, black sororities, men's groups, and church congregations are evident. When there are black candidates for public office, they are likely to be elected, usually with the largest number of votes. In their elected role, these few black men and women seem wary of any issues that may touch, or reflect on, blacks in the community. Very few blacks in Columbia choose to juggle publicly a position as black and as policymaker.

It is possible to observe the difficulty of this kind of dual role when the black community services director must defend a CA staff policy such as the closing of the teen centers. He is quoted in an article in the *Columbia Flier* of June 5, 1974 called "New City Teens":

> CA doesn't have "a magic answer" to the question of what programs are best for teens . . . Columbia has not done very well in providing for the needs of any of its minorities, teens included. Recreational facilities . . . "are geared to the 3.2 family in its own home." Cultural and background differences are rarely taken into account. This, he notes, can be disconcerting to those who come from the city to Columbia and find things missing. He cites late night basketball playing by city teens as a case in point. . . . Teens are becoming another of the city's displaced minorities, he said.

This statement illustrates an increased awareness on the director's part that he must publicly acknowledge blacks in Columbia as his informal constituency. There are strong criticisms covertly conveyed in this passage that resemble the complaint of blacks mentioned earlier: "Columbians simply refuse to accept that there is a black community." He points out that Columbia "has not done very well in providing for the needs of any of its minorities," and that "cultural and background differences are rarely taken into account." That this statement will be understood by both blacks and whites as a public acknowledgment of black needs and interests testifies to the strength of this language of pluralism that obviates open discussion of race.

There is a second pattern suggested in this passage. If there is a political consciousness on the part of blacks in Columbia, it tends to define its mandate as the protection of the rights of lower income (and, by implication, black) residents. The idea that this minority is being overlooked is present in such phrases as "those who come from the city to Columbia," and "late night basketball playing by city teens." Despite the fact that fewer subsidized housing residents lived previously in cities than nonsubsidized housing residents, these phrases are understood as euphemisms for lower income black youth.

Except for a very few individuals, blacks have chosen neither to participate publicly in the decision-making process nor to offer something definable as a black community to be a source of legitimacy for those who make up the formal political structure. The monitoring of key controversial issues in order to identify the persons that appear around them and the attempt to demystify the private language in which the issues are argued in order to discuss power negotiation in the community seems always to bring us to the same category, lower income. Both blacks and whites, then, play out a sub rosa competition with symbols that define the arena as a class struggle.

There is a barely perceptible third pattern here: the definition of what it is to be culturally black is being taken from behavior that has not heretofore been associated with middle-class blacks. In the process, what little political activism is engaged in by middle-class blacks benefits the entire category of lower income, both black and white. This will become more evident in the two remaining case studies that concentrate on this critical intersection between being black and being poor.

NOTES

1   *Columbia Times*, February 7, 1974
2   Columbia Association 1973

5

POOR AND NONPOOR

THOSE KIDS FROM SUBSIDIZED HOUSING: CASE FOUR

In an article in the *Columbia Flier* of November 8, 1973 Theresa Garbus, a Columbia resident and clinical psychologist who had contracted with the paper to research and write a series on Columbia schools, discussed her observations and conclusions about the Steven's Forest and Swansfield elementary schools. The articles were critical of both schools and pointed to a gradual return to a traditional, structured form of education in the midst of carefully designed, innovative, open-space physical facilities.

A flurry of letters defending each school followed the publication of this article, and signalled a breach of the unspoken agreement about what is and is not talked about publicly. In the middle of each article were several sentences that removed the cover on the ideological container of class sentiments for a few days. These passages, in particular those about Swansfield, interpreted remarks made by school and volunteer personnel in the following way: the children of Swansfield's three subsidized housing developments (Abbott House, Waverly Winds, and Ranleigh Court) present management problems, and "don't care about learning, and need to be handled in a certain way to make sure that they don't get the upper hand." Further, it was inferred that school personnel felt that the kind of education generally accepted as part of open schools (less structure and more self-motivation) will not work with lower income children, and therefore more traditional forms of education are necessary in all of Columbia because of the presence of lower income families. The author concludes: "Columbia is soon going to have to decide whether 75 percent of its school population has to be repressed to contain the other 25 percent."

These articles raised a furor that raged for three weeks, and then the subject returned to its former place underground. A letter from a white resident of federally subsidized Ranleigh Court appeared in the *Columbia Flier* of November 15, 1973, and said in part:

> I am saddened to see that even the president of the Swansfield PTA can be classified among the benevolent blind. Can she really believe that "all" the problem children in Swansfield School live in Government housing? . . . I would hope that Ms. Buchanan makes a public apology to those people who stand to suffer by her thoughtless remarks and prejudices, . . . [and she should] get out into the world a little, and learn that all residents of Interfaith and Abbott House are not complete failures as providers and parents.

A public meeting, called by the manager of Waverly Winds (one of the three subsidized projects in the Swansfield school area) was held at the Longfellow Neighborhood Center on November 14. Invited were the principal of Swansfield, the president of the Swansfield PTA (to whom the questionable comments in the article were attributed), and Garbus; of these only Buchanan, the PTA president, was present. Approximately 50 parents from the two Interfaith sites affected attended. These residents had asked the manager of the Interfaith Housing Corporation to chair the meeting. Buchanan spent some time trying to convince the audience that it was Garbus's distortion of her remarks that was responsible for the impression that lower income residents were being treated as a special group. Buchanan continued to maintain that it "definitely doesn't matter where a child comes from at Swansfield," and that children with learning or management problems can "come from any neighborhood." Because Garbus was not present, it was difficult for these parents to move beyond Buchanan's denial of what had been attributed to her in the article. The parents were vehement that a meeting with all the implicated persons was needed, and Buchanan offered the regularly scheduled PTA meeting to be held on November 26. In closing, Buchanan urged each resident to bring a friend and suggested that one of the Interfaith residents fill the vacant post of PTA vice-president. There were angry murmurings of paternalism among the Interfaith parents, black and white, as they filed out.

Two letters were published in the *Columbia Flier* prior to the November 26 meeting. The first, from Buchanan, was an apology to the outraged parents:

> After meeting with a group of parents and realizing their deep concern about the social injustices too frequently directed toward residents of Waverly Winds, Ranleigh Court, Fall River Terrace, Abbott House, and Tilbury Woods, I want to apologize to all our parents for providing Ms. Garbus any information which led to her conclusion that any group of students at the Swansfield Elementary School is responsible for the school's basic educational approach.

Garbus's response to Buchanan was printed below this statement:

> I think that Swansfield is particularly fortunate to have you as its PTA president because you are so articulate and *responsive to community opinion*. . . . I think the residents of low and moderate income housing are being cheated when they are given the same approach and the same program (in more luxurious wrapping) that they had before they came. And to use their presence, as various administrators have done, to condone the overemphasis on discipline is a cop out.

Garbus did not attend the PTA meeting on November 26, so the same impasse in allocating responsibility for the offensive remarks existed as at the first meeting. After lengthy questioning from the audience was fielded by Buchanan, the Swansfield principal, a middle-aged black man, rose to respond to a resident who questioned whether 25 percent of the Swansfield student body was lower income as the article had asserted. The principal spoke with controlled anger: "I have 57 percent white, 40 percent black, and 3 percent Oriental in this school, and I could care less. The teachers don't even know where the kids live, and they could care less. . . . The children are doing what you don't have the courage to do—the children *have* to work in this mixed school. It is a challenge; it is not easy because people are different. I am not necessarily talking about ability."

The norms about what one can say in public about socio-economic mixing, and by implication about race, were broken in this case. The lid was quickly put back on, but the events that occurred before this could effectively take place are instructive. The residents of subsidized housing know that these kinds of statements are common parlance in private, but they will not tolerate public categorization that is unfavorable to them as a group. More important, they seem to have the power to stop it. It is notable that the black principal was able to raise the unmentionable issue of race directly and to say in other words almost exactly what Garbus wrote in the article: It is not easy in this school because people are different. A public incident such as this occurs infrequently because the ideology of racial and socioeconomic harmony keeps these kinds of sentiments under wraps. Covert, unfavorable categorizing of lower income residents is common, although in Chapter 7 it will become evident that the power of lower income residents to demand that they not be objectified and treated as nonpersons is increasing.

CLASS IN COLUMBIA

The achievement of a socioeconomic balance is somewhat less important to the Columbia ideology than racial openness. On the other hand, racial integration in housing has been achieved while the goal that 10 percent of all housing should be for families of lower income status fades as a probability daily. The idea of a class mix thus needs to be kept alive, to be protected more vigorously. In the survey discussed earlier, 17 percent of the respondents felt there were too few subsidized dwellings in their neighborhood, 11 percent the right amount, with only 13 percent responding that there were too many. There were no subsidized units in the neighborhoods of 22 percent of the sample. Of these, 41 percent responded that units should be built in their neighborhood, and 64 percent of these said the "Columbia ideal" was their reason for feeling this way. Given the level of fear that accompanies socioeconomic mixing in American society in general, this attests to the remarkable pervasiveness of the Columbia ideology on this issue.

Aware of the difficulties inherent in attitude survey questions that touch on sensitive issues, I have concentrated a great deal of attention on the identification of attitudes that are expressed more or less openly by physical and verbal behavior in the community, using nonobtrusive methods that have been discussed fully in previous chapters. There is a perceptible uneasiness about the residents of subsidized housing, and a striking lack of knowledge about who lives there; in fact very few Columbians who live in nonsubsidized housing have ever been inside one of the units. A letter to the *Columbia Flier* on November 15, 1973 from a resident of subsidized housing forthrightly addresses this uneasiness:

> I am a long-time resident of both Columbia and Interfaith Housing. From this rather unique position, I have frequently experienced and witnessed the economic prejudice of the average homeowner in Columbia against "those people in subsidized housing." . . . Actually, some of us really have it on the ball. We even have a few college degrees in our midst. Some policemen, firemen, county employees, nurses . . . the list is long. . . . I challenge the *Flier* to come—write an article—help us expose the people in "subsidized housing" for what they really are. Actually, you'll find us average Americans—and anyplace else we may even be considered middle-class!

What this resident points out is indeed the case; a very small number of these residents, black and white, are on welfare, and many are white-collar workers. Other myths are persistent and have very little basis in fact. Some of these have been touched upon previously: the idea that there are more children in subsidized housing than in Columbia in general,* that the black population in this housing is at least 80 percent, that the roots of crime in Columbia lie in these developments, that the lack of concern of lower income residents (and by implication, blacks) with the condition of their homes will lead to a decline in property values. The latter is of immense concern, and statements such as "Columbia will become a ghetto is we don't force those people to keep up their property" are often heard. Just such an issue will be developed as a case study in Chapter 6.

There are actually two sets of data we can talk about here. One set provides us with a picture of who the residents of subsidized housing are,† and the attitudes and beliefs they express about their

---

*No doubt this myth is fostered by the fact that a large percentage of the children in subsidized housing is black, even though the mix of households is about half and half.

†It should be recalled that only about half of Columbia's low to moderate population live in subsidized housing.

experience in Columbia (gathered through examination of existent survey materials and with the use of nonobtrusive methods). The second data set reflects the ideas middle-class Columbians have about the class mix; in particular, it centers on what they say in real situations where issues arise that touch on the area of subsidized housing. At least two areas of discrepancy become evident, both of which are critical for an understanding of the dynamics of socioeconomic mixing in Columbia. The first of these is the incongruity between the facts of the subsidized housing experience for those who live there and the beliefs of the community in general about that experience. The second is the discrepancy between what people support as the ideal image of their community (equality by class, particularly in terms of equal access) and the reality of their experience.

The letter from a subsidized housing resident quoted earlier lamented the fact that Columbians have a whole host of misconceptions about "those people who live in subsidized housing." There are ways to fill in the lines of these "nonpersons": first is the Columbia Association survey,[1] which allows comparison of subsidized and nonsubsidized residents in Columbia; second, there is my own data, drawn from 18 months of focused attention on the five sites of subsidized housing built and operated by the Columbia Interfaith Housing Corporation. Meetings of the Interfaith board of directors, on-site resident meetings, and a considerable amount of time with the problems, both financial and social, of management have provided a thorough knowledge of this particular subsidized development. Although my in-depth knowledge is limited to Interfaith housing, demographic characteristics and personal knowledge of other subsidized units give reason to think of Interfaith as sufficiently typical to allow generalization in some areas.*

There is a widespread notion that residents of subsidized housing are very different from middle-class Columbians. There is no doubt that median income and occupational level are substantially lower for subsidized residents, and there are several other interesting differences, as noted in the forthcoming table.[2] The percentages in the table are based on a random, stratified sample of 1000 households; 52 of those interviewed lived in subsidized housing.[3]

---

*The self-management plan of Interfaith is, no doubt, a critical difference in determining type and level of interaction. I have not overlooked this.

	Subsidized	Nonsubsidized
Percent white	60%	84%
Earn less than $8,000	54%	5%
Belong to husband/wife household	52%	80%
Have two or more cars	17%	62%
Work outside of Columbia	59%	73%

Although in some ways subsidized residents are indeed different, their similarities to Columbians living in nonsubsidized housing are striking and generally not known.* Even the most knowledgeable people in the community were surprised at the similarities that emerged when the neighborhood survey materials were tabulated and compared. There was, for example, an impressive resemblance in the percentages of subsidized and nonsubsidized residents who came from metropolitan areas (in fact, more subsidized residents lived previously in suburbs than nonsubsidized), are satisfied with Columbia, were satisfied with their previous residence, find it easier to call on neighbors, believe race relations are better, think there are about the right amount of people of the same social background in the neighborhood, are not at all active in community affairs, and believe people like themselves have some or a great deal of influence in Columbia decision making. This may be a testimony to the relative meaninglessness of the survey questions; nevertheless, we can see that some of the questions being considered seriously by new town planners and analysts today elicit virtually the same response from both sets of respondents.

What can be said about the residents of Interfaith based on close observation? Even though these are rental units, the percentage of Interfaith residents who participate actively in the self-management program resembles that joining in the activities of relatively active, nonsubsidized townhouse associations. The concerns expressed and

---

*There is a striking difference between subsidized residents of Columbia and all residents of other nearby political jurisdictions: 75 percent of subsidized residents in Columbia have high school diplomas, while that number for Howard County is 60 percent and for Baltimore City 34 percent.

argued about at these meetings are similar for both: maintenance, child discipline, Christmas decoration, snow removal, and the like. There are similarities in the number of units improved with flowers and bushes (although subsidized housing plantings are generally more modest), the variation in child-rearing habits between strictness and permissiveness, the number of children per household, the density of social networks within the development, and the enthusiasm for a development-sponsored social event (yard sale, picnic, and so forth).

Little effort would be needed to calm the anxieties of middle-class Columbians about the threat of the different values of subsidized residents. Except in a very few cases, that effort is not expended.

THE SLIDING SCALE OF PAYMENT

Columbians do, however, spend time addressing issues about the welfare of subsidized residents. The sliding scale of payment is a concept that exemplifies this concern. A letter to the *Columbia Flier* on July 4, 1973, directed attention to neighborhood pool costs and the effect on lower income residents:

> In the five years that we have lived in Columbia, the neighborhood pools, which I would characterize as the single most universal recreation facility, have been made less accessible to the less fortunate through an average 16 percent yearly increase in membership fees.

This is an example of resident stimulation of the press to exercise its potential for legitimating CA decisions. At a Columbia Association executive committee meeting that followed the publication of this letter by one week, the CA director of commercial operations discussed a possible sliding scale of payment (until then limited to early childhood education) for neighborhood people. He pointed out that "only 10 percent of subsidized housing residents are members of neighborhood pools, compared to 50 percent of Columbia as a whole." He went on to say: "We need to find out why *they* are not joining *our* pools. There may be reasons other than cost; for example, that they don't feel welcome." He justified the cost of this subsidy by reminding the CA executive committee: "This decision will only produce income in that these people are not joining now."

Summer 1973 was the beginning of a more public social awareness about the possible exclusionary effects of user-pay charges for facilities and services in Columbia. There was before this time a sliding scale for day care and a plan for recreation facilities whereby community work earned credits toward "free" membership. During that summer, however, the process of examining facility and service policies for these exclusionary effects grew rapidly. As it did, the prospect arose of a head-on collision within the community. Individuals and groups, some committed to providing more than just a place to live for lower income residents and individuals,* and some reluctant when it became clear that subsidizing lower income residents would necessitate trade-offs in terms of issues that related to property values (such as open space maintenance), were in covert opposition. As one anti-day-care Columbia Council representative put it, "If we are to adopt day care as a policy, we must fund it so that every child in Columbia is accommodated; by doing that you won't get your grass cut."

I witnessed the widening of this breach in the community and monitored it closely through the 1975 fiscal year budget process. Day care emerged as the arena in which the split was played out, and as the cover-up for the real issue of whether or not Columbians wished to take steps to follow through on the ideology of equal access to facilities and services for all residents.

DAY CARE AS A "MALIGNANT MOSS"

By utilizing day care as the point of combat, it was possible to cope in the public arena with the issue of economic stratification without directly confronting it. Discussions became hopelessly mired by confusing the social and financial implications of a day-care subsidy policy with the possible detrimental effects of day care on young children. One executive committee member said, "Day care is growing like a malignant moss; we will be overrun by it." When economic exclusionary practice was the issue under discussion, lengthy and convoluted debate invariably ensued about what income levels should be subsidized and to what extent. These debates shied

---

*The Columbia Association was one of these groups. The CA staff, for both political and genuinely altruistic reasons, is committed to this goal.

away from centering on defining the goals of a sliding scale policy and concentrated on issues such as resentment that "families earning $16,000 a year do not pay full costs for baby-sitting." (It is important to note here the attempt to switch arenas from economic policy to the value of day care by inserting a negative connotation to day care with the word baby-sitting.)

At this point CA staff and community policymakers were caught between two opposing forces. They had designed the sliding scale of payment in a manner that they thought would avoid negative reactions from moderate income families about the inequities of subsidizing only those of an arbitrarily defined category, namely, lower income. The opposite happened: community sentiment centered on the idea that families with "plenty of money" were being subsidized instead of debating the importance of the policy per se.

Often the economic and social issues were submerged in debates about the appropriateness of day care "if it is not an absolute necessity for the mother to work to support the family." One unfortunate result was the fragmentation of the early childhood education lobby. Cooperative nurseries, because they represent low costs to the community, became the favored alternative. Little recognition was given to the obvious inconsistency between emphasis on cooperative day care, where a parent contributed time on a regular basis, and meeting the needs of working mothers. There emerged a consistent and growing feeling in the community that CA should be redefined "as a facilitator rather than a provider of services"; that is to say, a facilitator, through provision of reduced cost space and modest subsidy, of nurseries and family day care rather than a total provider. There were problems with this approach. The only way CA could withdraw from the provider role and still subsidize the lower income families would have been for higher income residents to pay more than full cost for services; any suggestion that this might be a possibility aroused widespread resentment.

At this point, a family day-care training program was brought forward as a move not only to maintain a commitment to day care and to the needs of lower income residents, but also to capitulate to anti-day-care, antisubsidy forces. The committed members of the day-care/sliding scale force viewed this as a "cop-out," and even more serious, as "in many ways a class issue." For example, they pointed out that noninstitutionalized family day care had been going on since Columbia began; why suddenly did there need to be training programs? I came to understand their uneasiness in the following way: a large policy change from institutional day care to family day care would mean more class isolation. Middle-class parents are not likely to seek family day care in lower income families, nor are they likely to see themselves as candidates for any sort of training program. Lower income people, on the other hand, have been caring for each other's children on a reciprocal basis all along; thus, training programs can only be viewed as another way to instill in lower income people the child-rearing values of the middle class. Further, two cost structures would emerge that would effectively protect the status quo: lower income parents would pay low rates to lower income caretakers, and higher income parents would pay higher rates to middle-class caretakers. However, nothing of the class argument was mentioned in the public arena; family day care was consistently discussed in terms of being a superior method of dealing with the problem of a mother having to work.

Columbians are fairly committed to the idea that their city must be something more than a racially integrated, but one-class, community. Their efforts to realize the goal of a sensitive, economically mixed community are evident in two ways. First, there is a continual discussion about the failure to meet the projected figure of 10 percent subsidized housing, and about ways, given the sharp decrease in federal support for low and moderate income housing, that the community itself could invest in providing more housing for families of limited means. Second, there is a concurrent and continuing debate about the means to insure that lower income residents will have access to the services and luxuries that life in this new town is supposed to provide. The debate about what is a service and what is a luxury is an interesting one; swimming pools, for example, are slowly moving in most people's minds into the service category, while tennis and health club facilities are still clearly luxuries. On the other hand, medical care is scarcely debated (although many worry about it) because the provider is in the private sector.* This means the issue of equal access to good medical care for families of limited means is "out of our hands."

---

*Those Columbia residents who choose to participate are served by a prepaid, closed panel, medical plan that is affiliated with the Johns Hopkins University School of Medicine and financed through the Connecticut General Life Insurance Company.

The case that follows provides evidence of a third aspect of this social experiment in class integration. At the same time that lower income residents are seen by the larger community as a category whose situation is different and whose "special needs" must be considered, lower income residents are coalescing as a category that can be viewed as an "informal political grouping whose operation is a fundamental part of the total political structure" of the community.[4] A series of confrontations over several years' time has been critical to the development of this category (lower income) as an instrument of power for enterprising politicians and for the people themselves. The next chapter will describe these incidents in depth, and examine the language of dispute for clues to the ways in which individuals manipulate the ideas and rhetoric surrounding class to maintain or change the distribution of power between categories of people. Conflict and confrontation will be analyzed to help uncover the dimensions of existing power relations, and to abstract from fairly mundane debate some hints to the changing relationships of power.

NOTES

1   Columbia Association 1973
2   Columbia Association 1974c
3   Columbia Association 1973
4   Cohen 1969:218

6

CONFLICT AND CONFRONTATION: AN EXTENDED CASE

INTERFAITH: THE EMERGENCE
OF AN INFORMAL POLITICAL POWER

It was a foregone conclusion that some organization would emerge in Columbia to carry out the commitment of James Rouse to build a city that was socioeconomically diverse. Rouse is a deeply religious man, and he fostered the idea that a religious group would be the ideal vehicle for this task. The first move to build lower income housing in Columbia came from the Roman Catholic Archdiocese of Baltimore; eventually the Columbia Combined Ministry (a Protestent coalition) and the Howard County Jewish Council were persuaded to join the effort. In June 1967, after several months of organizational efforts, the Columbia Interfaith Housing Corporation held its first meeting. The Columbia Combined Ministry, representing 13 major Protestant congregations, and the Roman Catholic Archdiocese of Baltimore agreed to expend equal amounts of seed money to conduct necessary studies and to make the other initial arrangements for the erection of approximately 250 units of federally subsidized housing. The Jewish Council of Howard County was designated as part of the sponsoring coalition in January 1968.

The corporation set as its primary goals to furnish housing at the lowest possible cost for families unable to find housing at the regular market rate, to scatter this housing throughout the community, and to make a contribution to the developer's goal of making Columbia a racially and socioeconomical open city. By March 1968 working capital had been raised, market analysis carried out, and preliminary drawings had been favorably received by the architectural review board of the Howard Research and Development Corporation (HRD). Successful negotiations for below-market purchase of five sites in Columbia were completed with HRD, and by June 1969 the builder had been selected, rough grading had started on three sites, and footings were poured at the first units. Services of the American Baptist Management Corporation (ABMaC) were retained at the time that the first units were occupied in February 1970.

Management under ABMaC was plagued with problems from the beginning, seemingly due to poor maintenance and interpersonal strife with residents (such as the way in which the management office notified residents concerning their delinquent rent). These difficulties between management and tenants led the Interfaith board of trustees to look for representation from residents as a way of checking on management. The composition of the board at this time was five appointees each from the Columbia Combined Ministry and the Roman Catholic congregation and one from the Jewish Council. The proposal was to appoint two nonvoting resident representatives. This action was described to me in the following way: "The Catholics suggested a young, middle-class woman whom they knew, and the board looked around for a second possibility. A resident of Interfaith who was at that time director of the day-care center in one of the sites was chosen. These two appointees attended board meetings for a while. Eventually they stopped; the young woman said that the board was condescending, used big words she couldn't understand, and so she quit." This meant the board was without resident representation during the period when drastic moves to cope with the financial difficulties of the corporation were being discussed.

These persistent problems were the impetus for a plan to increase rents and to separate the cost of utilities from rent payments, charging residents with the responsibility of gas and electric charges for their respective units. This decision held two serious potential problems for lower income residents: first, the proposed change would increase monthly costs to residents by more than 25 percent;

second, each resident would be required to provide an initial security deposit in order to continue receiving the utility service previously carried by the corporation. Residents began to organize in an attempt to convince the corporation that this charge would impose an intolerable hardship on many Interfaith families.

The *Bulletin Board*, a resident newsletter created early in 1972 and designed to be "a means of communication between the Residents, the Management, and the Board of Directors," provided an important vehicle for residents to share their discontents about actions of management and the board. In this case it served to gain support for residents as they tried to stop the board's proposed rent increase and the separation of rent from utilities. There are several references to this policy decision in the May and June 1972 issues of the tenant newsletter. An editorial on the first page of the May issue stated:

> We feel we must voice loudly the fact that in truth, most of the residents who have spoken to us are *not* happy with either a rent increase or a rent decrease plus utilities. Much protest was made over the decision of the Board, mainly due to the fact that although there are two spots on the Interfaith Board for resident representation, there has been *no* direct representation for some time. At *no* time were the residents made aware of any possibility of a deficit in the Budget which would make personal payment of the utilities necessary. Several petitions were circulated, and a letter was sent to HUD and the Board asking for a freeze on the entire matter until an investigation could be made. At this point the letter remains unanswered. At this time we are very disappointed in the entire matter, and feel . . . that the residents are not being treated fairly or in a decent or humane manner. Wasn't [Interfaith] built for the *residents* originally, and what has happened to that concept?

A series of meetings between board members and residents occurred over these months when the rent increase problem was brewing. Referred to as "a historical first," a number of board members and residents met on April 18 to "make clear the feelings of all concerned with the scheduled rent increase." At this time residents elected a committee, with at least one representative from each site, to be a liaison with the board. On April 22 this committee met in emergency session with the executive committee of Interfaith to discuss input from the Department of Housing and Urban Development (HUD). Following a directive from the regional HUD office, the rent increase scheduled for May 1 was suspended, and the utility separation was set for June 1 with a corresponding rent decrease (in an attempt to compensate for the increased costs to residents in this policy change, HUD ordered that rents be lowered). Further, a promise was extended to residents from the board that "all structural defects which could result in high utility bills will be repaired as quickly as possible."

On June 9 a well-attended meeting of residents considered a proposal from one member of the resident committee to accept "the payment of utilities and set up strong tenant organizations that could be used to put pressure on the board to fix our houses." Residents did not receive this proposal favorably and voted to continue to fight the utility separation policy. On June 14 four board members met with 150 tenants. These board members announced that a donation from a prominent builder in Columbia would be used to help pay the security deposit required for individual utilities for any family who found it financially difficult, and promised to expedite repairs of weather-stripping and window caulking.

An open letter to the June issue of the *Bulletin Board* gives some indication of the growing resentment of the board among residents:

> As a resident, I wish to make an effort to award a DOUBLE BLACK EYE of the month to two Board members who have consistently attempted to replace God in our lives. They have undertaken to harass and threaten residents, invade privacy, interfere with residents' business, and remove our Constitutional right to a Free Election and fair representation. They apparently feel that because we don't have much money, our intelligence is limited also. The Resident Liaison Committee, originally a good idea, too late in coming, seems to be becoming a "rubber stamp" of the Board—thanks to the pressure that these men have been able to apply. When is the Board going to get up off their apathy and do something about this unbelievable situation?

The Interfaith Corporation's board of trustees were all members of the socially concerned middle class. At this time they represented a wide range of occupations and orientations: a local builder, a planner for the archdiocese, a black Columbia minister, a retired political figure in Howard County, the vice-president of the National Urban League Development Foundation, a senior vice-president of the Rouse Company, and a former priest (at this time in real estate) who was the first president of the corporation. The attitude of these members toward their tenants had been one of well-meaning benevolence (members were sufficiently aware to remark negatively about "the Christmas basket mentality about the poor"). The attitude of "respect for the poor" that prevailed was a rather thin veneer, however, and the issue of tenant responsibility for utilities effectively stripped it away. Hostility was rampant on both sides and, as conflict is wont to do, threw into relief the basic power configurations between the corporation and the tenants.

Residents became aware of what they considered deep-seated condescending attitudes on the part of board members, and of their own powerlessness in the face of these attitudes. To illustrate these attitudes, the president of the corporation was quoted in the press as saying: "People who are complaining . . . feel the world owes them a living. Maybe it does, but not in this society." Tacit denial of serious defects in the construction of Interfaith continued in the face of a great deal of evidence to the contrary. When my investigation of this situation began I was assured by two of these board members that "these residents are going to be able to reduce their heat bills. It's their African ancestry that makes them want to have the heat at 80 degrees. They'll change fast enough when paying their own utility bills." Attitudes such as this added to growing resident discontent. One resident appeared angrily before the board to say: "This Board really needs to do an about-face before it can begin to deal with problems. You need to wipe yourself of the pious attitude of messiahs or redeemers of your downtrodden brothers."

Several months of accelerating tensions between tenants and board, together with increasing financial marginality of the corporation, led the board to consider a more effective scheme of representative tenant membership. The organization of the resident community in opposition to the rent increase also served as the major catalyst for this change. It was decided eventually that a committee of five residents (corresponding to the physical sites) would be elected and entitled to two votes on the board. However, when the board petitioned for résumés of interested residents, only two individuals responded. This raised a flurry of controversy on the board about the absence of due process that placing only these two residents on the board would entail. Nonetheless, it was resolved in favor of accepting these candidates (Joseph M. Marshall and Georgia Goslee) as full voting members, and at a meeting in June 1972 the board ratified them as Group II Trustees.*

This marks the first appearance of Marshall in the informal political circles of Columbia. At this time Marshall was known as an innovative and sensitive nursery school teacher, running the only Summerhill-type early childhood education program available in the community.† His ascension into a strong position as power broker in the community was steady since the time when his résumé was submitted to the Interfaith board of trustees. In the early spring of 1973 he was hired to manage Abbott House, a lower income project just built by a subsidiary of the Rouse Company. In short order thereafter he was elected to the Harper's Choice village association board of directors, proposed the on-site management plan for Interfaith, and was hired as coordinator (in effect, manager) when the plan was adopted. He was later elected president of a newly formed corporation designed to address low- to moderate-income housing needs in all of Howard County and suggested as an independent candidate for the Howard County Council.†† Although Marshall is middle class in background and education (he grew up in the New York City suburbs in a middle-class Catholic family, attended Fordham University, and was just short of a bachelor's degree at the University of Maryland when he became involved full-time in antiwar activities), his residence in lower income housing and his anti-middle-class lifestyle (he could flaunt a tattered army jacket and jeans even at formal occasions) were crucial to his role as representative of lower income residents. His position as spokesman for the needs of this group was accepted by residents of Interfaith, by the Columbia Association staff and executive committee, and by the press.

To return to the history of the Interfaith Housing Corporation,

---

*Group II Trustees had been established some time earlier when the president, a Catholic priest, left the priesthood and married a member of his congregation. His importance in the founding of the corporation stimulated establishment of a category of board members who would be nonreligious appointees.

†It is worth recalling that early childhood education is an extremely political area in Columbia. It is quite possible that involvement in this area was instrumental in raising Marshall's consciousness about the potential power to be garnered.

††A short while after this research was completed (spring 1975), Marshall ran successfully for the position of Columbia representative. Follow-up investigations indicate that for some period of time he continued the sorts of activities reported here from the position on the executive committee of the Columbia Association.

we have seen that the board ratified Marshall and one other volunteer (a black female law student.) as representatives of the Interfaith residents in June 1972. In July these two residents distributed copies of a document that recommended, among other things, an increase in the tenant representation on the board. This document read in part:

> The committee discussed the need for establishing a tenants' advisory body and reached the following conclusions: that the problems currently existing between the residents of Community Homes* and the board of directors are and have been the result of a gross lack of communication. . . . When the tenants have been asked for counsel it has been or has appeared to be with the arrogance that the middle-class has traditionally reserved for their seeming emotional and intellectual inferiors—the poor. . . . To serve any useful function and to guarantee the required support for the residents, the committee would have to be given certain real power, the particulars of which will be discussed in this committee's recommendations. . . .

These recommendations were mainly about increased responsibilities to residents: to deal with resident relations in the courts (such as eviction), to determine policy for the physical maintenance of the grounds, and to determine policy for the newsletter (the board had attempted to interfere at the time of the rent increase). In a separate section the recommendation was made to increase tenant representation. The first section of the report was passed at the same meeting at which it was presented. During the period of time when the expansion of resident representation on the board was being explored (eventually to be resolved by having three categories: Group A, the religious appointees; Group B, a representative from each housing site; and Group C, nonreligious, at-large community representatives), Marshall was nominated and elected to be assistant secretary-treasurer. This meant that a tenant representative was now a member of the executive committee of the corporation.

In March 1973 Marshall submitted his resignation as tenant representative on the board because he was moving from Interfaith to a similar sized unit in a moderate-income apartment complex in

---

*Interfaith Housing was originally named Community Homes, but this has never gained wide usage.

Harper's Choice.* He had accepted a new position as manager of the recently completed subsidized high-rise project, Abbott House, and "had a lot of time to spare." Some of this time he spent developing an on-site self-management plan for the five sites of Interfaith. The major features of this proposed arrangement were: termination of the management contract with American Baptist Management Corporation; appointment of a qualified person as coordinator of the plan; hiring of a resident as part-time manager and maintenance person at each site; and organization of an elected on-site committee for each site to make policy and financial decision for that site. The plan was designed to funnel more than $30,000 annually back into the community in part-time positions for residents in management and maintenance. Marshall, just recently resigned from the Interfaith board, was named to the position of coordinator of the five separate operations. The president of the corporation announced the adoption of the plan to residents as a solution to the financial difficulties of Interfaith. "We are operating on a skeleton budget, but raising rents is not the solution," he said, and continued by describing the plan as based on "the idea of spreading more participation and control of operating dollars" to the residents, and of "giving decision-making powers to the residents."

The design and implementation of this plan, then, lay with Marshall. The specific details were approved by the board at a special meeting in March 1973. At the same meeting Marshall was confirmed as coordinator of the plan, and it was voted to terminate the management contract with ABMaC.

This was an extremely innovative step for the board to take. At first I was given the impression that this change had been effortless and welcomed by the board. As I began to make my way through the minutes and correspondence of the corporation, and widened my contacts within the community, it became increasingly clear that the decision to adopt Marshall's proposal had been very difficult. The doubts about the wisdom of this approach, although hidden quite effectively at first, were still alive, just below the veneer of a "corporation *of* the people." When two of the original founders of the corporation explained "the importance of this venture in self-

---

*Marshall's election to the Harper's Choice village board coincided with this move. Although it is not required that village board members live in the village represented by the board, it is obviously a sound political move to do so.

management," they spent most of the interview congratulating each other on how adventurous they were to have entrusted Interfaith "to someone like Mike Marshall." It became evident that there was still a great deal of insecurity, as one of these original founders told me, about "turning the corporation over to a hippie." There were essentially two reasons why the board was willing, albeit somewhat reluctantly, to take this step: first, ABMaC was predicting financial disaster and the possibility of going into receivership within the coming year; and second, the two resident representatives were always badgering the board with complaints from residents about management and the dearth of resident input to policymaking on the board. Thus, the board was faced with a dismal picture about ABMaC management whenever they said, "Let's hear what residents have to say," and with constant catastrophic expectations whenever they heard from ABMaC. The prospect of "another tenant rebellion" was all too real.

In the midst of potential disaster for this venture in lower income housing in Columbia, Marshall appeared with a carefully considered plan that claimed the financial problems were the result of uninspired management, incorporated innovative procedures for involving tenants in the management of the housing, and therefore seemed likely to head off the feared tenant revolt. Although there was considerable opposition to the idea of residents controlling the on-site budgets, Marshall convinced the board that turning the money over to residents could not possibly be worse than the situation had been with a professional management organization. The two board members most vocally opposed to the plan (the Columbia builder and the black Urban League official) resigned shortly after the action was taken to approve the plan.

The question then arose about whether Marshall should remain on the board in his new capacity as employee of the corporation. At a subsequent meeting he made it clear that if he were not placed on the board in some capacity he would resign as coordinator. The opposition to Marshall's insistence that he be a trustee was worded in terms of "the conflict of interest that would appear in the case of a paid employee serving on the board of trustees." Marshall was adamant, however, and with a great deal of in-house politicking between the time of this meeting and the subsequent one where the issue was voted upon, the position of coordinator was added to that of the at-large Group C trustees.

POWER REORGANIZATION UNDER NEW LEADERSHIP

A conflict between Columbia Interfaith Housing and the Roslyn Rise Day Care Corporation arose in the month immediately following Marshall's appointment as coordinator and member of the board. Both corporations were in severe financial difficulty at the time Marshall began his tenure. The immediate crisis concerned the renegotiation of the lease that had established Roslyn Rise Day Care as tenant of Columbia Interfaith Housing for the nominal sum of one dollar per year. When Marshall took over the management in May, he spent a great deal of time familiarizing himself with the corporation files. When he examined the original lease that the two corporations had signed, it became clear that the intention was that the Interfaith Corporation should not bear any extra costs in the course of housing the day-care facility. This agreement had been gradually eroded; for example, the day-care group was not paying for water charges. Moreover, the situation had become a heavy drain on the Interfaith housing maintenance staff, who often spent as much as half of their working hours dealing with recurrent breakdowns of plumbing facilities and various other problems that are common in facilities serving young children.

During the period when he lived in Interfaith Housing, Marshall was a resident of the Roslyn Rise site. This, along with his experience in early childhood education, meant that he had considerable knowledge about both the operation of the center and residents' opinions of the service provided, as well as an interest in "straightening out some of the problems about who pays for what, and excessive maintenance calls." In his first month as coordinator, Marshall approached the director of the day-care center with a request to meet with her board to discuss some of these problems. At this time there was no suggestion of changing the one dollar a year rent; Marshall wanted only to reestablish the original "sense of the agreement" that Interfaith should not be carrying extra expenses because of the day-care center. He found that the day-care board of directors "didn't want to deal with me." It was at this point that the controversy began to expand.

The Interfaith board was also concerned with these pragmatic problems. The monthly financial reports indicated that the center was a drain on resources, and rumblings had been going on for some months that "the day-care center is too expensive." A fiscally conservative member suggested at the June 1973 board meeting that the day-care group "has not reported to the board with any regularity." Marshall responded that he was in touch with the director of the center and the president of the Roslyn Rise Corporation concerning this issue. Indeed, as we have seen, he was involved in preliminary informal attempts at negotiations that were proving to be far from fruitful.

The history of the mutual involvement of these two corporate actors required a necessary digression here. In April 1970 the Interfaith Corporation executive committee and the Columbia Combined Ministry executive committee recommended that a committee be formed of representatives of the two Interfaith sites then occupied and of the three sponsoring denominations of Interfaith Housing, with additional members experienced in early childhood education. The committee was charged with making recommendations for the best use of the multipurpose space available at the Roslyn Rise site, and was incorporated as Interfaith Day Care Centers, a nonprofit organization. Attempts to raise seed money were instituted and the possibility of a supportive role for the Columbia Association was explored. In August 1970 the executive committee of Interfaith Housing agreed to lease the multipurpose space in Roslyn Rise to the group on a one-year, automatic option for renewal basis. This space had been designed originally as a gathering place for Interfaith residents, and was the equivalent in space of two one-bedroom apartments. The corporation further agreed to expend $8,700 to insure that the facilities were in compliance with the Health Department requirements for a day-care center, and to lend $2,000 in seed money to the day-care group. In December the first classroom was opened with 19 children, and by May 1971 there were 38 children enrolled in the center, 26 of whom were from Interfaith families. In the fall of 1971 the corporation agreed to expand the space to accommodate a kindergarten half-day program along with the two nursery classes.

There were recurrent references to a possible subsidy from the Columbia Association during this period. It was finally agreed that CA would subsidize the building of the playground and provide maintenance support and transportation of the kindergarten children between public schools and the center. No program subsidy was ever successfully negotiated, however. The financial burden of the very low tuition children* was eased somewhat when in August 1972 the Howard County Department of Social Services began funding the care of children from families on welfare; however, a private day-care center with a heavy marketing approach picked up 30 of these 50 welfare slots, cutting deeply into the amount of subsidy the Roslyn Rise board had anticipated. It was thus a time of severe financial stress for Roslyn Rise when Marshall approached them about the lease renegotiation.

In the process of the informal negotiations mentioned above, Marshall discovered a little known fact that was to prove crucial to the position of the Interfaith board. Roslyn Rise served approximately 40 children in its kindergarten and day-care programs; of these, at the time during the summer months when he queried the director of the center, only six were from Interfaith families.

This loss of Interfaith families reflected the residents' reactions to two issues. First, although Roslyn Rise had a sliding scale that insured a reduced charge for lower income families, the center was expensive compared to sharing child care with the neighbors, especially for families with more than one preschool child. The novelty and ownership of the center attracted Intertaith residents at first, but the relative cost became apparent after a few months. Second, it was reported to me that the whole process of income certification to qualify for reduced tuition carried an implication of "we're doing this for you." Parents of Interfaith children found participation on the Roslyn Rise board unsatisfying and the attitude of "the do-gooders" condescending.

When it became clear that informal negotiations were at an impasse "because the day-care people refused to consider the seriousness of my concern about the costs being borne by Interfaith for operation of the center," Marshall attended the August meeting of the Roslyn Rise board. At this meeting Marshall formally presented the following recommendations he intended to make to the Interfaith Housing board concerning the renegotiation of the lease with Roslyn Rise:

- Include water charge and rent in the lease;
- Remove from the lease the large storage space;

---

*Roslyn Rise Day Care's sliding scale allowed lower income families to purchase full day care for approximately $10 a week.

- Include maintenance specifications in the lease;
- Keep written records of all dealings between Interfaith and Roslyn Rise;
- Submit the center's annual financial report to Interfaith.

The meeting was civil and low-keyed, not at all the tone of the members of the day-care center's board when not in the public eye. While maintaining a reserved and refined demeanor during this meeting, these members, in private, acknowledged that they were outraged at Marshall's behavior. At one point Marshall suggested that non-Interfaith families utilizing the center pay a small surcharge with their monthly tuition. "They wouldn't even talk about it," he reported.

It was this seeming lack of concern and unwillingness on the part of the Roslyn Rise board to consider seriously the alternatives that led him to recommend to his board the imposition of a substantial rent. He pointed out that not only was the day-care center incurring expenses for the corporation in utilities and maintenance, but also half of the space could well be utilized as the main Interfaith office and thus free a two-bedroom townhouse (the present office site) for rental. At the same time, the other half of the space could be used for community service (mental health counseling, thrift shop, or the like) or could be rented for additional income to the corporation.

Marshall calculated the cost to Interfaith residents of the space in question, based on square footage and normal rental rates for apartments and townhouses in the complex. On this basis he proposed by letter to the Roslyn Rise president a monthly rent of either $385 that would include full maintenance, or $265 that would not. The day-care president attended the October 1973 Interfaith board meeting to present Roslyn Rise's case; namely, that they could not possibly afford to meet the above terms. "A few months ago 40 percent of the Roslyn Rise children were from Interfaith Housing," he said. The Interfaith president emphasized that since only six of the presently enrolled children were from Interfaith, the residents were in effect subsidizing day care for the rest of Columbia and for many families with substantially higher incomes. A motion was passed to ratify the terms Marshall had proposed to Roslyn Rise.

It was at this point that Roslyn Rise turned to the Columbia Association and the Early Childhood Education Board (ECEB) for assistance. These two organizations played small but significant roles in this controversy. During the planning process for Columbia, emphasis was placed on innovative early childhood education; an early childhood education board was approved by CA in September 1970. Any qualified member of any village association was designated eligible for membership. In effect, two persons with expertise in the area are appointed annually by each village board. Precisely because early childhood education represents a very active relationship between CA and the community, studies of political process often come to rest at the intersection of the roles of CA, the Early Childhood Education Board, and the village boards.

In this case, Roslyn Rise approached CA for aid, either in the form of financial assistance or in the form of CA space at a nominal rent. Marshall was confident that CA, because of the heavy constraints of the ideology that Columbia is a community for "all kinds of people," and the history of this day-care center as a vehicle to provide care for lower income children, would rescue the situation either by paying to Interfaith Housing the rent on behalf of Roslyn Rise or by providing another space for the facility. This seemed a no-lose situation to Marshall. Either Interfaith would get a substantial sum from CA as rent on behalf of Roslyn Rise or the center would vacate the space for CA space, allowing its use for other income-generating purposes. An important point is that Marshall and the Interfaith Corporation did not have to worry that Roslyn Rise would go out of existence because of its actions. CA, with the advice and consent of the Early Childhood Education Board, ultimately decided to offer the CA-owned Bryant Woods Children's Center to Roslyn Rise.*

COALESCING STRENGTH OF LOWER INCOME RESIDENTS

This conflict is an illustration of the increased awareness and manipulation of the category lower income resident in Columbia.

---

*Although this would necessitate another case study in itself, we might point out that CA was utilizing the Early Childhood Education Board to advocate a policy that CA favored to the Wilde Lake village board. The Wilde Lake Cooperative Nursery would be displaced by this proposed relocation, an action that would surely arouse the ire of some of the citizens of Wilde Lake. Thus, as discussed more fully in Chapter 2, CA needed the advance support of the ECEB in order to legitimate this policy decision. Moreover, by moving the Roslyn Rise program to a CA facility, the Bryant Woods Children's Center, CA was strengthening its day-care statistics in a fiscally conservative year without direct cost to the community.

Interfaith Housing and Roslyn Rise Day Care, since their inception, were corporate bodies of equal status in the eyes of the community and of each other. Each was a corporation of public-service status, established to provide a service to lower income residents; one, housing, and the other, day care. The legitimacy of private service organizations is rarely questioned in our society. There is an unspoken rule of hands-off that governs the relationship between organizations of this type. It is simply not fair play for one public-service organization to question the legitimacy of another concerning the appropriateness of the service it performs or the degree of competence with which it carries out its task (assuming that it operates within some broad standard of competence). During this period, *Interfaith resident* was not very identifiable as a category, and there was little input by individual residents to the policymaking of either corporation. Thus the status of the residents in relation to both Interfaith and Roslyn Rise was one of recipients of services.

As a result of tenant organization to oppose the rent increase, several changes in this state of affairs took place. First, the residents of Interfaith gained a sense of self-awareness and corporate potential they had clearly not obtained before the proposed rent increase. The circulation of petitions, collection of information about heating costs of individual units, publication of the newsletter, and election of representatives to the board encouraged a recognition of an Interfaith community. Second, this incipient corporateness held within it the threat of tenant revolt, and as a result there was a change in the rules of the games between the corporation and the residents. Previously, the power of the corporation rested on that legitimacy inherent in its public-service role; it was, after all, providing housing to people who presumably would have difficulty obtaining other suitable housing. When the residents publicly questioned the humaneness of the corporation (and thus, in American ideology, its competence), the Interfaith Corporation's legitimacy became problematic.

The corporation dealt with this problem with a series of moves: increasing the input of residents to the board, instituting a self-management plan that would funnel rent monies back into the community, and hiring an Interfaith resident as coordinator to the board. Besides restoring the legitimacy of the board, these moves changed the source of this legitimacy. The increased resident input and membership in the corporation made it a corporation *of* the people, "representing the poor," rather than one that simply provided needed services.

Some choices were made here that are important to point out. The board chose to take some extremely innovative and risky steps (such as self-management) to avoid the possibility that this growing sense of corporateness among the residents would undermine its legitimacy to the point of causing serious malfunction (for example, a rent strike). The residents, on the other hand, chose to surrender the potential power they might have had as a corporate body with an active tenents' council when they were offered the above improvements. The option for both groups to have available this kind of choice is a mark of pluralism. As is often the case in pluralistic communities, each chose to invest in a power broker rather than risk a breakdown in the system.

That broker was of course Marshall. At the time that his proposal was adopted and he was appointed coordinator, he was a fledgling in Columbia politics. This reorganization and his appointment to administer it were of critical importance in his rapid consolidation of power and his option to act as broker in this situation of developing pluralism. Before this time his power lay in the intelligent and articulate representation of his constituency: lower income people and apartment dwellers in Columbia. The appointment as coordinator widened his options for categorical affiliation; property management as an occupation carries with it all the accoutrements of the middle class, and a certain amount of instant status. His source of legitimacy, as is often the case of a "middleman"[1] in power struggles, was bidirectional. Powerful individuals at CA, among his village board colleagues, and among policymakers at HRD were more respectful because of his position as manager of Interfaith, and the confidence and respect of the Interfaith board of trustees was more easily won because of his position among these powers in the community.

Because Columbia is a community where the ideology supporting socioeconomic integration is powerful, the corporation was strengthened by this change in its source of legitimacy to one of representing rather than serving the poor. Interestingly, while it seemed to imbue the corporation with a feeling of power that allowed it to question the legitimacy of the Roslyn Rise Center, the incorporation of a resident as coordinator and member of the board seemed to affect negatively the Roslyn Rise board members' assessment of the legitimacy of Interfaith. It was the outrage of these members, seemingly all out of proportion to the facts, that first called my attention to this case. Ths Roslyn Rise board members remained totally uncooperative in the face of specific details about the lack of participation of Interfaith families in the day-care program and the extreme financial distress of the corporation that was penalizing the Interfaith residents when it incurred debts that did not directly reflect benefits to the Interfaith community. The Roslyn Rise board was adamant that it was the personal irresponsibility and greediness of Marshall that was causing the problem. There was every indication that the day-care people ignored Marshall's early attempts to reach a solution that would not strain either corporation unduly precisely because they categorized him as a lower income resident, associated this with powerlessness, and therefore failed to consider his approaches seriously.

The course of the conflict was relatively independent of the strength of the Interfaith board's case. Although it certainly helped to be able to establish the unfairness of the present arrangement to Interfaith residents, the Interfaith board would not have been able to resist community pressures against "throwing these children out into the cold" if the norm governing the relationship between the two corporations before the Interfaith tenant revolt ("middle-class charitable groups may decide what services lower income people need without interference from one another") still prevailed. The change in this norm brought about by the self-management plan (to one of "lower income people themselves are the only ones to decide what services they need") allowed the Interfaith board to question the legitimacy of the Roslyn Rise board.

A CHALLENGE TO CULTURAL PRIVILEGE

In the summer of 1974 another crisis arose when the architectural committee of Wilde Lake denied proposed changes to the play areas in Rideout Heath, one of the five sites of Interfaith Housing. A three-year effort by residents of Rideout Heath to improve these facilities in their community, having received informal approval from CA staff and formal approval from Howard County, was turned down by the architectural committee. Although no specific reasons were cited in the denial, a series of confrontations followed by a formal meeting between members of the Interfaith board and the architectural committee clarified what had not been overtly stated before: the architectural committee intended to use the playground issue to improve, in their words, the "appalling maintenance" of the two Interfaith sites in Wilde Lake Village, namely, Rideout Heath and Roslyn Rise.

Some considerable time before this crisis occurred, the residents of Rideout Heath, the largest of the Interfaith sites, had begun planning for improvement of the play equipment at their site. A letter in the June 1972 *Bulletin Board* states:

> The playground in Rideout Heath is a disgrace. . . . Compare our playground with others in Columbia. They are well-equipped with sturdy wooden structures resting on soft, SAFE moss or sand. Don't our children deserve the same?? Must they be condemned to a summer in the dangerous areas provided for them to play? Let's do something—before a child is hurt.

Rideout Heath was originally equipped with the standard sort of gray tubular steel swings and slide. The residents were interested in two major improvements: they wanted "attractive" and "imaginative" equipment similar to that found in all locations in Columbia except Interfaith communities, and they wanted the equipment scattered at several locations throughout Rideout Heath to reduce the number of children playing in one area and the consequent effects of soil erosion and annoyance to residents living immediately adjacent to the equipment. It had been a long process, contingent along the way on such things as volunteer professional design assistance, concept and budget approval by the CA, and approval by Howard County. The Wilde Lake resident architectural committee had been involved at each step in this process, and although the composition and authority of this board had recently changed, the appearance of the on-site manager for Rideout Heath at a hearing for approval of the final plans was considered by Interfaith management as a pro forma exercise.

Much to the dismay of this on-site manager, the session became, in her words, an "outright attack." Interfaith management was accused of "appalling maintenance" and "spendthrift attitudes." The application was officially denied without cause being formally stated. Informal communication, as well as less direct statements, made at this hearing indicated that the issues foremost in the minds of the committee members were maintenance levels not up to the "standards of the rest of Columbia," and the "appropriateness" of the community expending monies (through CA) on play equipment when "there is already perfectly good equipment on the site."

The rights and obligations accompanying the authority of the architectural review system are important here. The documents setting these forth make provision, among other things, for the composition of an architectural committee and for general and specific covenant restrictions. Architectural committee approval is required for the following kinds of actions: any exterior alteration, landscaping, or screen planting over two feet tall, construction of any structure (for example, a storage shed), installing of playground equipment, painting house or trim in a color different from the original, or erecting any fence or awning. Moreover, the following kinds of actions are prohibited: putting up either a television antenna or clotheslines, erecting a sign, parking a trailer or camper in public view, and storing items such as garbage cans in public view. Regarding maintenance, these documents say:

> Each Owner shall keep all Lots owned by him, . . . in good order and repair, including but not limited to, the seeding, watering and mowing of all lawns, the pruning and cutting of all trees and shrubbery and the painting (or other appropriate external care) of all buildings and other improvements, . . . (Section 6.01).

In a handout given to all new residents, this statement appears:

> Each resident should keep his property . . . as is befitting of the concept of Columbia. Only with the help of all of the residents can the Architectural Committee assist in maintaining the total environmental qualities of the new city of Columbia and enhancing the worth and appearance of each property.

At the time that this conflict erupted, Wilde Lake had reached the end of the development period where a changeover had just recently taken place from a resident/volunteer architectural committee with ultimate responsibility in an HRD-designated architectural committee, to a Columbia Association/village association controlled body. Because of this, there were several characteristics of this newly formed body that may have effected the manner in which this conflict unfolded. First, this was a milestone event in terms of the history of Columbia and, in particular, Wilde Lake. It marked the beginning of the gradual move toward resident control; specifically, it was the first time that residents (as appointees from the village and from CA) held authority with formalized (and in this case, legal) legitimating mechanisms. The press, for example, described the newly formed committee during this period of crisis as "overzealous" (*Columbia Flier*, August 15, 1974). Second, as the committee was new, the members had had very little time to work out interaction problems among themselves. Third, all of the preliminary negotiations and understandings in the case had taken place between the Rideout Heath residents and the previous resident architectural committee.

This system, although fully legal and carefully designed to spell out the rights and obligations of both the architectural committee and residents, allows considerable leeway for the selective interpretation of rules. As one village board member said disdainfully: "Some village boards view the covenant advisor and the resident architectural committee as instruments of social control." The more generally accepted roles of the architectural committee are two. First, its members act as advisors to those residents who wish to change the exterior of their property in order to "maintain the total environment qualities of the new city." Second, but not less important, is its role in enforcing the restrictive covenants. It is in this area that there is potential for wide variation among architectural committees.

There seem to be two basic models for enforcement procedures that are evident when one spends time observing the meetings of the various architectural committees. The first of these is the mediator model, where a village architectural committee steps in when a complaint is filed and seeks to facilitate an amicable solution to the conflict. These types of conflict can occur between individuals (for example, if one individual moves an air-conditioning unit away from a bedroom window to a location that is annoying to a neighbor), or between collectivities (for example, when a townhouse association seeks to build a fence between its complex and the neighboring apartments, as in Case Two above). In other words, under this model an architectural committee "does not go around looking for violations." The opposite of this model is the aggressive enforcer role. Architectural committees clearly have available to them the power to function in this manner (Sunday afternoon tours around the village to look for violations of the covenants exemplify this approach). The different village committees do not invariably function in one or the other manner; rather, the models represent a continuum, and a committee usually conforms to a norm that is well beyond the midpoint in one direction or the other.

The next confrontation in the playground case occurred when the architectural committee appeared one Sunday morning at Rideout

Heath. I received a call from an informant and arrived in time to observe the last half of the interaction between members of the committee, accompanied by the one black member of the Wilde Lake village board, and representatives of Interfaith Housing including Marshall in his capacity as coordinator and overall manager and several residents. A general "trashy" environment (cans, loose papers), bare spots without grass, and a few serious erosion problems represented the first of the committee members' complaints. Both the wording and the tone of the conversation were patronizing and hostile. "Appalling filth" and "lack of responsible management" were repeated often until Marshall, up to this point adopting an attitude resembling a citizen receiving a visit from the police for breaking the law, appeared to lose his temper. He began to return their remarks in a similarly aggressive tone, pointing out the financial difficulties of the corporation and the limited amount of money available for maintenance compared to a profit-making complex in Columbia. The members responded with increasing hostility to his demeanor, but the nature of their complaints changed subtly. "Look at the condition of these backyards compared to those," they said, indicating the Cross Fox luxury townhouses next door. Indeed there was a striking difference; while the yards of Cross Fox residents contained generally expensive and attractive lawn furniture and barbeque equipment, Rideout Heath residents tended to have snow tires, lawn mowers, and trash containers.

Committee members focused on the "responsibilities of subsidized residents" at this point. "Those people should be out here every day picking up trash," and "Why don't they appreciate the privilege of living in Columbia?" are characteristic of the remarks from the committee.* They seemed totally uninterested in Marshall's discussion of the financial realities of most of the families: single-parent working mothers, both parents working, men with two and three jobs. He pointed out that Interfaith had been forced to spend an exorbitant proportion of its budget (which, he made clear, was totally composed of tenants' rent monies) on heating and air-conditioning problems due to faulty construction, that Interfaith units

---

*It seemed at first that the black member of the village board was not going to side with Interfaith management. Her point was quite the opposite of those expressed above, however. She maintained that Interfaith residents were not getting what they deserved from management. As the conflict intensified she eventually sided with Interfaith management.

have no basements or other storage areas, and that residents tend to spend more effort fixing up the inside of homes than the outside. His argument had two parts: first, the corporation was doing the best it could possibly do with maintenance given its financial limitations; and second, under no condition would he accept the imposition of middle-class standards of aesthetics and cleanliness from this committee. Although the group moved on to inspect Roslyn Rise, the other Interfaith site situated in Wilde Lake Village, an impasse seemed to have been reached; discussion languished, some half-hearted compliments about the attractive flowers around some units were offered by the committee, and a date for a meeting later in the week was set.

This meeting, held at the home of one of the architectural committee members on July 8, was attended by essentially the same parties. Much of the tone of the meeting echoed that of the Sunday morning site visit; namely, hostility on the part of committee members (with one attempting to play a conciliatory role), and alternating cooperation and resistance on the part of Marshall. A new issue arose: these members were "also appalled" with the fact that new equipment was to be installed at all, and "shocked" that the on-site manager had replied in answer to questioning at an earlier meeting that she did not know what would happen to the steel play equipment that was being replaced. When Marshall responded that an on-site manager would not be expected to know what the corporation might do with this equipment, and that there was "a history in this request for tot-lots that this committee has not been a part of," the committee maintained that it could see no reasons why the present equipment was inadequate. It was suggested that "if the parents are concerned about better equipment, why aren't they concerned about open garbage and general trash?" The group was at another impasse and adjourned with both parties concurring (with quite different expectations, as will become apparent) that the issue should be discussed further when members of the Interfaith executive committee could be present.

This meeting was held on August 5 with the entire architectural committee and its administrative assistant. Attending from Interfaith were the president (a mortgage banker), the treasurer (a certified public accountant), the secretary-treasurer (highly respected in political circles and at that time a likely candidate for Howard County Council), the Rideout Heath on-site manager, and Marshall. The editor and general manager of the *Columbia Flier* was also present. The chairman of the architectural committee began with a statement that was conciliatory in tone:

> We are concerned that Columbia continue to be a good place to raise our families. . . . We are looking at areas that have not been maintained as well as they could have been. . . . We want to make you aware of areas to be improved, suggest some of these improvements, and pinpoint some areas where you need help. If you need help, we are prepared to help. What is needed is an overall plan. . . .

The president of the Interfaith board responded by offering to "give a rundown" on Interfaith in terms of its inception, organization, and finances. There was no response. He went on anyway:

> There is a common misconception that Interfaith is public housing. This is not true—rather it is part of federal program 221 (d) (3); the only help from the government is a reduction in the mortgage rate from the then 6% to 3%. Rents are however fixed by the government. . . . We guard the purpose for which this housing was established very dear. . . . We took over fourteen months ago from a former attitude of "we-they" stance to a "we" stance. All our residents don't have the energy or the interest, however.

One of the more hostile members of the architectural committee asked, "What makes some people want to meet the standards of Columbia and some not?" Another remarked again, "We need a plan to bring these projects up to Columbia standards." There was some movement to end the meeting on the part of the committee when the Interfaith president pointed out that the issue "we came here to discuss has yet to be brought up—the tot-lots at Rideout Heath." After several comments from committee members about needing information on the disposal or further use of the present equipment, the Interfaith treasurer responded: "When I applied for permission to install new equipment in my yard you didn't ask me what I would do with my old sandbox." The Interfaith president pointed out: "We have to face the serious disappointment on the part of residents who have spent a great deal of energy on this plan." At this point the chairman appeared to sense that the discussion was not going in the direction he had planned, and ended the meeting with a request that Interfaith management submit a statement advising the committee about plans to control erosion, maintain the new equipment, and dispose of present equipment.

Between the time of this meeting and the formal reconsideration of the application, and following an informal interview of Marshall by the press, an editorial directed at the architectural committee appeared in the *Columbia Flier* (August 15, 1974). To quote in part:

> Village architectural committees usually do not go around the city looking for problems. They usually do not act as a sanctioned vigilante group, ferreting out covenant offenders. . . . Allowing public authorities to selectively interpret rules—of whatever legal status—is an obvious danger to a democratic system. It leads to abuse of these "laws," to their use as harassment, social control and as an outlet for personal bias and prejudice . . . the architectural committee is apparently "blackmailing" the Interfaith residents. Having taken upon itself the unsolicited task of assessing the quality of maintenance at the two Interfaith properties in Wilde Lake, . . . the committee members have decided the upkeep there is "appalling." Now if everyone was always required to comply with the letter of the covenants, the Wilde Lake architectural committee would have a stronger basis for imposing its maintenance requirements on Interfaith, but this is not the case. . . . The "standards of Columbia" the committee is so bent on protecting include a great deal more than land maintenance. They have to do with dignity afforded people and understanding of financial realities and the value of cooperation. . . . A messy yard doesn't look half so bad for Columbia as does self-righteousness, insensitivity and bigotry.

During this same period, statements responding to the three points mentioned by the committee were cursorily added to the original application by Marshall (for example, "the equipment will be maintained in good order with appropriate amounts of mulching"), and resubmitted. Contacts made by Marshall with the administrative assistant to the committee led to "inside information" that only two of the five members of the committee were determined to "bring Interfaith up to the standards of Columbia," and that efforts were being made to review the resubmitted application while these two members were out of town. This review came up on August 19, and one of the "difficult" committee members attended unexpectedly. He attempted to block the approval of the plans on the grounds that the item had mistakenly not been published as part of the agenda.

He received no support, however, and the motion to approve passed. There was no further communication about this set of maintenance problems after that time. A diagram of the complex set of relationships in this particular case appears in Figure 6.1.

This case is an example of almost imperceptible but steady social change in a heterogeneous community. As the conflict is played out, we can watch the architectural committee attempt to use, one after the other, the categories of "we" and "they" that have been part of the structure of middle-class configurations of power. There are no simple answers to why they failed. There are, however, some important clues to how the rules of the game are subject to inexorable shifts when people are forced to confront the discrepancies between the ideologies they profess and the public acitons in which they engage.

When the residents of Interfaith were confronted without warning with what in effect was a 25 percent rent increase, two processes were set into motion. The shocking realization of the exorbitant heating costs of the units, and the attempts to gather information among themselves to buttress their case to the board and to gather supporters among residents spawned the first effective organization of the Interfaith community. Newsletters appeared, communication between sites became commonplace, and most important, leaders began to emerge within the community who would not be "intimidated by middle-class society."

In this case, the architectural committee opened the controversy with a demeanor of superiority. Marshall's dress did not set him apart from the community he administered, and the committee chose to interact with him on this basis rather than as a middle-class equal active in policymaking circles. It was a serious tactical error, and Marshall, with his intuitive understanding of the advantages to be gained by maneuvering people into making public statements that are at odds with the ideology professed in the community, manipulated this choice to Interfaith's advantage. By adopting an air of subordination in the first stages of the site inspection, he encouraged committee members to display their power. The stance of the committee as protectors of the accepted value system of all Columbians except lower income residents was out in the open. Words like "filthy" and "appalling" were used over and over and the committee became entrenched in the position of "forcing the poor to be more like us." Once all the derogatory words and phrases had

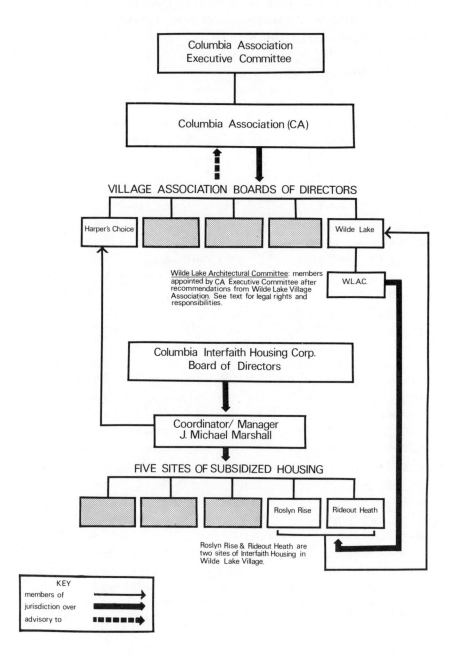

been uttered often enough that the committee could not retreat from having said them, Marshall became the articulate middle-class property manager, arguing from the position of a hostile equal and barraging the committee with highly technical financial details. He thus switched his affiliation from the "they" category, in which he had allowed them to temporarily place him, into their self-defined "we" category. At the same time, however, he refused to accept their definition of the shared value system of that category.

The committee was thrown off balance by this maneuver, but it took another meeting between the same parties before they realized the intractability of Marshall (for example, "it is impossible to talk to him"). At this point the committee suggested a meeting with the board of trustees, assuming that these two bodies of middle-class volunteers would be able to talk to each other because they shared an interest in the community. When we demystify these phrases, we find the committee expected that "the standards of Columbia" would represent a shared symbol between the two bodies. To be able to talk to each other implies an unspoken agreement about what key phrases mean. "An interest in the community" subsumed just such an unspoken agreement; namely, a primary interest, not in the Interfaith residents' well-being, but in the effect of this federally subsidized housing on the property values in the area.

It was a clever move; the architectural committee had every reason to believe that a meeting with the board would lead to a gentleman's agreement reflecting a general understanding that it was to every property owner's advantage that Interfaith "look good." The rhetoric with which the architectural committee chairman began this meeting should have cancelled out the adversary impasse that had been reached with Marshall. The chairman could have expected that the Interfaith board would direct Marshall to cooperate, even though the committee was aware of the difficult public position into which they had been maneuvered by Marshall (that their interest lay more in the looks of the development than in the well-being of its residents). They hoped to save face if the Interfaith board agreed.

It is not surprising, given the general lack of knowledge in the community about Interfaith, that they failed to predict correctly the power configuration between the board and the coordinator. Members of the board did not openly acknowledge that the power had been conveyed to the coordinator and that their role was solely one of legitimating his decision-making authority; in fact, however, the board did not direct the coordinator except in instances where he sought their direction in order to assure shared responsibility. This had been a slowly evolving process, marked by changes in attitude of some board members and gradual replacement of resignees with individuals more interested in the welfare of residents than in the image of Columbia. The board members knew that if they failed to support Marshall in a public issue (or any issue on which he chose to take a stand), he would resign. Although another manager might be found, it would have been difficult to replace Marshall's ability to maneuver advantages in the community for Interfaith residents (from CA, for example, where he convinced the commercial operations director to provide a package plan for recreational facilities at less than half price for these residents).

The committee saved some face by pretending that the issue all along had been one of the potential maintenance of the new equipment and by insisting that Interfaith carry out the empty exercise of resubmitting the application with information to this effect. Marshall did this reluctantly after the board convinced him that it was a small concession. The manner in which he addressed the questions clearly conveyed his derision for the committee's "persecution" of Interfaith.

PLURALISTIC INTEGRATION AND POWER BROKERAGE

When I began to monitor the Interfaith Housing operation on a regular basis, shortly after the self-management plan was instituted, Marshall paced like a caged lion and was unable to eat before board meetings. Within a year's time he was totally at ease in the situation. The Roslyn Rise controversy coincided with these early stages of his administration of Interfaith, while the issue of the Rideout Heath play area fell at the end of his first year of tenure as coordinator. The process of power consolidation that is reflected in these coincidences warrants a further look.

When Marshall began to establish his political entrepreneurship, he had substantial experience as a resident of Interfaith and as a spokesman for these residents. He had, in other words, legitimacy in the role of lower income representative. The quick disappearance of the protest accompanying the rent increase suggests this; certainly the board received no letters protesting his election as they did earlier about the board "fix" of the resident liaison committee. Very shortly after this time the Interfaith residents chose Marshall to chair the controversial Swansfield school meeting where, it will be recalled, they intended to confront the personnel of a local elementary school about the unpleasant categorizing of their children in an interview with the local press. There is a common thread that ran through every informal interview I carried out in the Interfaith community. It can be paraphrased by the following statement: Mike may not do everything right, but he deals with us as intelligent equals and we know he is with us.

On the other hand, at the time when Marshall took over Interfaith this sort of legitimacy, secure with residents, still had to be built up with the board and with sectors of the community at large. His strength in the Interfaith community had thrust him into the management role and into the local political scene (the largest bloc of votes for his village board position was from Interfaith and from lower income apartment dwellers in general), but his ability to be middle class was not yet established. Predictability is a component of power; at this point Marshall was an unknown and unpredictable entity to political Columbia. If we look at the Interfaith case study as exemplifying the developmental stages of this process, the capacity for mutual prediction as a critical component of pluralism can be seen. For example, in the case of the day-care controversy, Marshall could risk precipitating a break with the center because of the no-lose situation where the ideology of the community meant that some organization would rescue the facility. However, some crucial elements of mutual predictability were not yet developed.

Each of these elements contributed to the final resolution. First, his tenure was so recent that the Roslyn Rise board members had not had sufficient time to understand the base of legitimacy that Interfaith residents afforded him. In fact, these members did not comprehend that lower income residents could be a potential source of legitimacy. Second, although Marshall had a good understanding of the realities of the financial trade-off process at CA, he did not predict, as he might have had he been in citywide politics for a longer period, that CA could use this conflict to its own advantage. In the early stages of this encounter Marshall fully intended to ask for a relatively modest contribution from Roslyn Rise, and then to be able to maneuver carefully so that this contribution would come to Roslyn Rise from CA, and thus to Interfaith as rent. Although this initial attempt to manipulate from a brokerage position failed, the final resolution (the vacating of the center) represents his growing ability to balance on the tightrope strung between constraints placed by the ideology on community decision making and the pragmatic concerns of his different constituencies. Third, it was necessary for him to expend energy on this case because his position on the Interfaith board was tenuous and new. Although several of the board members were anxious to end the financial drain of the day-care center, the pressure against evicting the group, viewed as an anti-social-policy decision by the community, was exceedingly strong. I was surprised when the board ratified his substantial rent proposal, and feel that this decision was the result of a laboriously established case for the welfare of Interfaith residents that the board simply could not ignore, even in the face of community pressure. Thus we see that the consolidation of a power brokerage is a difficult process; one must initially put a tremendous amount of effort into developing each potential source of legitimacy. Judicious choice is necessary; there are traps to be avoided, such as calls from the high school about problems with teenagers from Interfaith. Accepting this kind of role would constitute paternalism, not brokerage.

The Rideout Heath playground episode illustrates this power brokerage at a later developmental stage. Although Marshall did not instigate this confrontation as he did the day-care case, he certainly was not unprepared for it; the "looks of Interfaith" has never been a dormant issue in Columbia. It took hardly any effort to dispose of this issue, however, because by this time he had his power base in order. Parenthetically, the architectural committee did have legitimate complaints; a general unkempt appearance and grassless pedestrian traffic-ways are normal at Interfaith. This is what some residents mean when they say that Marshall "doesn't always do everything right." Nevertheless, he makes choices about how to expend the limited resources of Interfaith (for example, on painting, heating and air-conditioning repairs, and well-paid employment for residents), and this case indicates his power to make these choices without interference from the community, and with the unquestioned support of the board.

It is important to look at how Marshall went about tapping the sources of legitimacy outside Interfaith. Rossi has pointed out that:

> Homogeneous middle-class communities, for example, dormitory suburbs and the like, will tend to have monolithic power structures, since the class basis for countervailing political power does not exist.[2]

The opposite of this structural situation exists in Columbia. As a hetergeneous community, it is marked by polylithic or pluralistic power structures, and each had to be manipulated by Marshall. More precisely, it was the gaps between these political structures that he needed to identify. This was a risky business; a middleman can sustain only a limited number of breakdowns between the powers he seeks to mediate without losing credibility. While pluralism is a necessary state of affairs for the establishment of a power brokerage, the cleavages and ties inherent in pluralism are a continual threat to the delicately balanced power of the broker. This is so especially during the period when the differences between categories are being institutionalized into the power idiom.

The task at hand for Marshall was to politicize class. Socio-economic integration was part of the ideological rhetoric of the community, and thus part of the social idiom. No doubt this made the task of institutionalizing class into a political idiom easier. Some might even object that it makes Columbia a unique situation that limits generalization. However, this same normative prescription is present in American ideology, even if more difficult to manipulate because of the complications inherent in the multiplicity of cleavages. The choice of Columbia, where pluralism is essentially composed of two classes and two races, means that the research site allowed me to control for a number of these cleavages.

What Marshall set out to do was to establish a core of mutual predictability between himself and the power sources in the community.* By the time he became coordinator this was largely accomplished with Interfaith residents and board. This does not mean that the relationship with the board did not need anxious nurturance for awhile; in fact, the groundwork was laid by the residents themselves, as shown above. By the time of the Rideout Heath playground case, however, Interfaith (residents, board, and coordinator) had become in many ways a corporate body.

The challenge for Marshall was in extending this legitimacy outside the boundaries of Interfaith. The beginning of his tenure as coordinator coincided with his election to the Harper's Choice village board. Although it may appear that he has been engaged in a series of planned actions to consolidate power on behalf of lower

---

*This predictability seems to be most successful because it is measured. People are never able to predict with total confidence, no matter how clear the outcome seems to be, which side of an issue he will take.

income residents (if not personal power), the actual sequence of events that have carried him along from one political move to the next are generated by the potential for pluralism inherent in the combined hetergeneity and ideology of the community. To illustrate, Marshall's campaign for a position on the Harper's Choice village board was stimulated and supported by extensive help from a Columbia Council representative from Harper's Choice with interests in both socioeconomic integration and housing needs for low and moderate income people in all of Howard County. Thus the coincidence of being elected almost simultaneously to the position with Interfaith and to one of the more influential political positions in Columbia was largely the product of other individuals' interests in bringing lower income residents into the political process.

Similarly, the press in Columbia is extremely sensitive to issues that may conflict with the ideology of racial and socioeconomic integration; as a source of legitimacy for Marshall it was invaluable. He often provided information and opinions in telephone chats with reporters that then appeared some days or weeks later in an article or editorial without attribution. For example, the *Columbia Flier* editorial on August 15, 1974 discussed the Wilde Lake architectural committee as "vigilante(s)" and instruments of "social control" who were "blackmailing Interfaith" with little regard for the "dignity offerded people and [no] understanding of financial realities and the value of cooperation," an almost direct quote of Marshall's remarks during one of these chats at which I was present. Thus Marshall could test ideas without having to accept responsibility or risk damage to the core of responsible leadership that was one of the chief supports of his role as broker. It allowed him to maintain an appearance of reacting to community sentiment, when in fact he was creating it.

It is unlikely that I was the only one who recognized this as a covert feedback system with the press. The architectural review system as an instrument of social control was an often mentioned shibboleth of Marshall's, and others must have marked an invisible hand in this editorial. Politically astute policy influencers in the community were no doubt aware of and respected the significant source of power afforded Marshall by the press, and yet were kept off balance by its sub rosa nature.

A comfortable stronghold of power from which Marshall ventured forth into his various spheres of influence was the Harper's

Choice village board. At the time this board was marked by a mutual respect and genuine liking among members. Nevertheless, Marshall could hardly have been more different. Philosophically, he was somewhat like the Columbia Council representative from Harper's Choice, who supported his candidacy and was committed to social concerns. Their political styles, however, were very different and at times in competition. Marshall was very careful not to strain his fellow board members beyond their ideological limits, a remarkable feat considering how conservative those limits would be without his presence. Without a hint of aggression or rancor, he was able to generate a role for this board as watchdog for equal access. In a sense, this issue became the glue that held this very divergent group of people together.

In no way, however, did this watchdog role resemble a political platform for the board; quite the contrary was the case. It was not a platform precisely because Marshall, while drawing the legitimacy for his power from successful brokerage, could not afford the risk involved in "coming out." His maneuvers within the board were almost unnoticeable; attendance at a series of the bimonthly meetings would provide a careful observer with little or no indication of the critical part he played in brokering for lower income people within the larger community. No doubt a gradual learning process transformed the perceptions of these board members so that the ears of each member became attuned to issues with potential for class discrimination, allowing Marshall to be just one of the group.

An example of this situation was observed nearly a year after this particular board had been working together (April 16, 1974). The issue being discussed was the sliding scale of payment for day care either run or monitored by CA and the Early Childhood Education Board. Several members of the board, without input from Marshall, were debating the income level at which CA subsidy should stop, and questioning whether the amount of subsidy should be higher for the lowest income brackets. Roslyn Rise Day Care was scheduled to move into the CA space form Interfaith, allowing public input into its rates and policies. One member remarked that it would not be necessary for CA to match the rates of Roslyn Rise in the lower brackets precisely because of the availability of the Roslyn Rise "bargain" to lower income families. Quietly Marshall interjected: "Having CA day care more expensive than Roslyn Rise for lower income residents says that we think the poor do not need a choice."

Eyes widened slightly, looks of "of course, why didn't we think of that" were exchanged, and a unanimous vote was taken to insure that Roslyn Rise and CA lower income rates be competitive.

Marshall had these four basic sources of legitimacy that he handled with great care: the Interfaith residents, the Interfaith board (these two so successfully that they are in some sense one), the Harper's Choice village board, and the press. The rest of the community he alternately badgered and cajoled with this solid power base behind him, expressing anger at "short-sightedness' and "fiscal conservatism at the expense of equal access." No doubt this was one of the reasons that "he didn't do everything right" at Interfaith; many hours during the working day were consumed paying calls on those in a position to influence or formulate policy. This represents a well worked out system that was at least partially understood by those Marshall badgered and cajoled, and he was used as a source of legitimacy, for example, by CA staff. In this reciprocal process, pluralism and the dignity and rights of lower income residents were served.

Power reflects a relation between persons rather than simply a resource held by an individual actor, and confrontation is one medium of communication between competitors for power. It is thus useful to examine public forms of competition under a fine lens, for they can provide "a limited area of transparency on the otherwise opaque surface of regular, uneventful social life."[3] Although Americans are homo equalis by ideology, homo hierarchicus is hidden in the rhetoric of the competition for the rewards society considers appropriate items for differential distribution (money, property, higher education, occupational status).[4] Examination of the language with which persons compete to maintain or increase the maneuverability they hold in a stratified society helps cut through the veil that our egalitarian ideology throws over the crucial principles that underlie our social structure.

The fault lines of social and cultural differentiation in Columbia may seem of minor significance amidst national events such as the social and political breakdown accompanying mandatory public school integration in South Boston. This book suggests, however, that the building pluralism of this planned heterogeneous city, set as it is in the present historical context of a nation experiencing an "extraordinary consciousness of competing identities and solidarities,"[5] can tell us things we very much need to know about the system of rights and obligations that accompanies the accumulation of privilege (that is, wealth and status) in society.

NOTES

1   Bailey 1969:167-76
2   Rossi 1968:137
3   Turner 1957:93
4   Dumont 1970
5   Fallers 1974:6

7

THE
POLITICS OF PRIVILEGE

A particularly violent episode with both race and class implications took place in Greensboro, North Carolina, in November 1979. The *New York Times* carried the following discussion some time after the event:

> Dr. Robert Doctor, a regional official with the United States Advisory Commission on Civil Rights, provoked a minor furor last week when he suggested that race relations in the community had been "in a tailspin" since the November shootings. . . .
>
> "It wasn't a racial matter at all," Mr. Smith contended. It was more a matter of class war than race war: four of the five Communists who were killed were white and two of those arrested for the shootings were themselves textile workers.[1]

These comments highlight a larger problem than one frightening case of inhumanity and hatred: they speak poignantly to the continuing confusion that surrounds race and class in American society.

WHOSE VALUES ARE THESE?

Being black and being poor have always been associated in the United States. Even with the expanded affluence of recent years, blacks represented a larger proportion of the poor in 1970 than in 1959.[2] This means that when attention is directed to less affluent Americans, the subject of race is often encountered. Moreover, the issue of socioeconomic mixing in neighborhoods and communities invariably raises the question of the viability of simultaneous racial and class mixing, usually with negative conclusions.

Previous studies have reached an impasse at this intersection of race and class because of an overemphasis on identifying the cultural values of a group or category of people. The values of the poor have been imputed to be a cultural attribute unaffected by the structural position of lower income people in a stratified society. This means, for example, that federally subsidized housing developments are opposed by prospective middle-class neighbors on the grounds that the values of lower income people constitute a threat to middle-class property values. One hears over and over about the ways lower income people "disappoint" more affluent neighbors: they do not appreciate the opportunity to live in decent housing, their yards are always messy, they have too many children, they allow the property to deteriorate, in fact, they systematically destroy it. It is also said that families fortunate enough to be placed in newly built, federally subsidized housing ought to show their appreciation by maintaining the property as if it were their own.

Viewing issues that have to do with simultaneous race and class mixing from a cultural rather than a political point of view has led to a continuing and not very rigorous debate that Ulf Hannerz summarized very well in his book about a Washington, D.C. black neighborhood.[3] Many feel, however, that the culture of poverty debate was won by those like Elliot Liebow who argued that the key to understanding the configurations of life-styles among the less well-off members of our society lies in a structural response to powerlessness rather than in a heritage of cultural traits.[4] In this view culture provides only the form of social interaction, and as such offers important clues to the underlying structural patterns. Others have discussed culture as a patterning of behaviors representing a series of repetitive choices or decisions.[5] This emphasis on structure has led to an understanding that if a category of people, in this case those of lower incomes, are faced with a continual set of constraints on the choices they make, a life-style that reflects these limited choices may be identifiable.

The continual inferences in the culture of poverty literature about how the poor are unable to look ahead (known among social scientists as an inability to delay gratification) lead Liebow to comment:

> But from the inside looking out, what appears as a present-time orientation to the outside observer is, to the man experiencing it, as much a future orientation as that of his middle-class counterpart. The difference between the two men lies not so much in different orientation to time as in their different orientations to future time, or, more specifically, to their different futures.[6]

Liebow's insights have been a powerful corrective to the direction that social science and the concept of a culture of poverty were heading before he got to know Tally and his street corner. This deceptively readable book points out that poor people are not a subculture with a different system of values; rather, lower income people are, as individuals, faced with a different and usually more limited range of choices in their daily existence.

The constraints that lower income people face in obtaining equal access to the goods and services that are highly valued in our society is only one part of the story. The second set of narrowed choices is in some ways more pernicious; namely, the coercion of the poor to make choices that are valued by middle-class society. These kinds of intrusions are as strong a reflection of the relative powerlessness of the poor in an affluent society as are the destructive systems of income inequality, residentail racial segregation, and discriminatory practices such as exclusionary zoning and red-lining. Not only must the less well-off members of our society make do with considerably less comfort and luxury than their middle-class counterparts, but at the same time they are expected to internalize certain ways of life that place them in a position of striving for things they can never have.

The field of housing provides a good example of this, though it is far from the only apt illustration. The well-established and widely shared importance placed on property ownership and property values in American society dictates that a goodly portion of a family's expenditures be earmarked for items of benefit to the image of the neighborhood. As members of the middle class, we manicure our lawns, fertilize and plant with zeal, and in general use the outside appearance of our houses as an important vehicle for keeping up with the Joneses. This status-maintaining behavior is costly in both time and money, and yet we find it annoying that lower income people choose, for example, to store snow tires in the backyard or on the balcony rather than in the living room. A mid-1970s Hollywood production called *Claudine* protrayed the frantic activity in one black household to hide the kinds of items middle-class families not only value but consider necessities (steam iron, television, rug) when the word is passed on the street that the social worker is on the way. This scene conveys the position of these people with a clarity missing in decades of research on "the poor." Middle-class people insist that the poor value the same things that they do, while at the same time insisting that they are not entitled to have them.

One of the most important reasons the myth of a culture of poverty has been kept alive as long as it has is that anthropologists and sociologists so often choose to study the less powerful categories of individuals in our society. While this can be partially explained by the emphasis most anthropologists put on cultural differences, an almost total neglect of middle-class value systems and life-styles suggests that racial, ethnic, or economic groups other than middle-class Americans represent deviations from some set of mainline values, and for this reason warrant investigation. Rainwater, for one, clearly disagrees with such a simple culture of poverty focus when he says, "the American underclass is created by, and its existence is maintained by, the operation . . . [of an] inequality-producing system."[7]

One researcher, taking the cultural perspective, has suggested that middle-class families actually want a different type of housing than the less affluent.[8] There does seem to be support for the conclusion that the less affluent value a somewhat different set of characteristics in housing, even when they have the financial means to make the same choices as middle-class families.[9] To conclude from this, however, that lower income families value the utilitarian aspects of a home while middle-class families desire large lots and privacy misses the point precisely because it accepts middle-class behavior as the norm. While it does seem clear that members of the middle class have developed a shared symbolic interpretation of residence as a differential marker of prestige within their culture, just how these meanings are conveyed from one individual to another and the importance of doing so in maintaining a class consciousness have been sorely neglected in the attempt simply to dichotomize these values with those of the less affluent. This has resulted in decades of public policy decisions that support and maintain these unexamined values of affluent America, with the concurrent interference in and manipulation of the life-styles of lower income people.

The connections between race and class continue to be a persistent problem to social scientists and others who are accustomed to viewing these categories as discrete entities. Two observations emerge when we look closely at the data on race and class in Columbia. First, the proscription on categorizing by race is more severe than that on categorizing by class. Thus the data are richer on the subject of class, and my inferences tend to have more substantiation. Nevertheless, it should be recalled that many people in Columbia who do not live in subsidized housing think that Interfaith is mostly black. This seems ample justification for making some associations between what people say about the residents of subsidized housing and what they do not say about blacks. Second, it is important to move beyond previous assumptions that these two categories can be defined by a set of cultural markers and contrasted to middle-class values as the norm. We need instead to pay attention to how the seeming confusion at this intersection of race and class is being used to exercise control and prevent changes in the traditional order of power and privilege in our society.

LOWER INCOME AS THE IDIOM OF MIDDLE-CLASS POWER

The question then becomes: Whose value system are we really talking about when we discuss life-styles of the poor or the culture of poverty? The key words and phrases isolated and analyzed in this book suggest that the continuing confusion may be due to the rhetoric of equality, more pronounced in Columbia but part of the fabric of American life. This rhetoric may serve in part as a cover for a system of privilege and control. Correspondingly, the culture of poverty may well be little more than a response to powerlessness and oppression.

The seeming contradiction in Columbia between the impression of an informal black constituency reinforcing racial solidarity across class lines and the fact that, whenever controversies or problems arise that seem to be related to race, "everything comes up class," is not a contradiction. Rather, it reflects the economic idiom in which power is being negotiated, an idiom that would suggest that the potential line of fragmentation is one of class. Most blacks in Columbia earn very substantial incomes; thus, they may be drawn by their class position to one political stance, and by their blackness or ethnicity to another. This kind of cross-pressured situation accounts for some of the cautiousness blacks exhibit. For example, there is no reason to expect that a middle-class black professional will find it easier to convince a group of hostile black youths to tailor their behavior to middle-class standards or to "go home" than a white person will. In some ways it may be more difficult for the black precisely because of his membership in two overlapping categories. Black policemen certainly face these kinds of ambivalent situations daily, and we can recall the conflict experienced by the black director of Community Services between his obligation to the black youth who regularly "hung" at Slayton House just before the demise of teen centers and his obligation to the Wilde Lake village board who wanted the youths thrown out.

Edmund Leach points out: "Esteem is a cultural product . . . an individual may belong to more than one esteem system, and these systems may not be consistent."[10] A strong emphasis on the cultural markers of blackness has not in the past been esteemed by white society. In fact, successful middle-class blacks have been under so much pressure to be culturally white that the markers of blackness whites know best are now strongly associated with poor blacks only. Many blacks were free to enter white society only if they learned to manipulate these two esteem systems with great skill. Only in rare instances, such as when James Farmer addressed a group of inner-city blacks on television during the urban riots, are whites reminded of these two separate and distinct esteem systems. White middle-class individuals usually forget that their suave and professional black acquaintances command two cultural systems equally well.

The cooperation between blacks and whites to maintain the power competition in a sub rosa state, with symbols that define the arena as a class struggle, may be illusory. It may only appear to represent cooperation; in fact, the choice of this idiom rather than one more openly associated with race may reflect quite different motivations for blacks and for whites. To illustrate, it is often mentioned that there were no racial problems in Columbia until

Interfaith was built. At first I dismissed this as the kind of uncomfortableness that middle-class suburbanites experience when faced with newcomers of different values. As I heard this statement more and more often and in totally different contexts, it became clear that there had indeed been some empirical changes in the community, but that blacks and whites had very different ideas about what these changes were.

The following kinds of comments were made by whites about the effect of opening the first units of subsidized housing. Teen centers began the process of racial separatism "after lower income people moved into Columbia." Black parents became hostile to white teachers, suspecting favoritism toward white students and patterns of underlying racism that were psychologically damaging to their children. "Outsiders" began hanging around in Columbia's village centers, and there were gangs that were not present in previous years. These were the changes white people murmured about in private, informal interaction.

Most blacks, when questioned, denied any changes had taken place. When probed, some sources suggested an entirely different set of changes. The Howard County NAACP has become more powerful, they said, and issues relating to racism in the schools, in hiring practices, and in police attitudes have been attacked more openly and vigorously. "Although the Howard County police are still racist, they are better and are making a sincere effort," one black man told me. Some blacks expressed the feeling that "things would have gone better between blacks and whites without poor blacks coming in," while another pointed out that the presence of lower income blacks has "freed up many blacks, especially kids, to act the way they want to."

It would seem that the presence of both lower income and middle-class blacks in Columbia has resulted in an informal, reciprocal gain for each. Since the white merchant can never be sure whether his black customer is a famous Washington lawyer or a janitor for the Columbia Association, he must treat all customers with equal respect. This is not only true of merchant/customer interactions, but of all informal interactions where no information is available about the participants in the interchange except diacriticals of dress, mannerism, and speech. For the janitor this means he is less likely to be the object of an implicating chain suggesting that being black and in work clothes means he is poor, and by being poor he is entitled to less respect. For the lawyer, the standard for proper behavior must no longer be based on the unspoken model of white middle-class values, such as conservative dress, careful diction, and reserved behavior. For both the result is more choice and fewer constraints. While the first informant was suggesting that without lower income blacks there would not have been tension and competition between blacks and whites because everyone would be interested in the same goals and would be willing to conform to the same value system in order to get them, the second informant pointed out that the choice of some model other than a white middle-class one was an important gain for all blacks, and that the entrance of lower income blacks into the community produced this choice.

From this it would seem that blacks and whites evaluate the link between lower income and race quite differently. Why do blacks cooperate to maintain a cover on race, and why do they choose, or at least participate in, the use of the cover that emphasizes class? This question risks the obvious pitfalls of discussing "what blacks want." In no way do I suggest that one may make generalizations about all blacks as a category or ethnic group; rather, I attempt here to pull out some patterns in order to shed light on the process of political collectivism of blacks that whites are encountering in Columbia. The blacks I have observed will not condone the negative categorization of lower income residents. Incidents where this stance is conveyed by a black have been observed often enough for me to feel that blacks in Columbia consider the less-privileged residents as a responsibility, and often as brothers. Moreover, in discussions where policy changes that would affect lower income people are the issue (I have described several in previous chapters), black elected officials are extremely careful to establish how much impact the changes will have on people in the lower income ranges; often this information would not otherwise be solicited.

In general, middle-class whites are not much concerned with the plight of lower income residents unless an issue surfaces publicly; for example, the issue that only 20 percent of subsidized housing residents belong to neighborhood pools, or that the "appalling condition of Interfaith units is turning Columbia into a ghetto." However, presentations about the details of the sliding scale of payment for day care of proposed plans for revamping teen programs are frequent and offer blacks the opportunity of a protective stance under the guise of class consciousness. Thus, there is a great deal of potential for covert political collectivism.

This evidence that blacks are choosing to coalesce as an ethnic category across class lines makes sense from both a cultural and a structural point of view. Most blacks in this country are less privileged than most whites. All blacks are to some extent oppressed in that they do not have the privilege of cultural (life-style) freedom. Many of those who have struggled into the middle class have done so by discarding, at least in public, a number of markers of cultural distinctiveness that have been retained by lower income blacks. In some sense, this leaves less-privileged blacks as the carriers of a cultural tradition that is now an important resource for boundary maintenance and ethnic identification as blacks gain strength as a political collectivity.

This is not to say, however, that we can expect middle-class blacks to foster the use of black dialect among their children. Rather, there is a deep respect among blacks for a variety of distinctive markers of blackness and for the freedom of each to choose those cultural markers that are comfortable and at the same time useful in self-definition. To provide an illustration: I suggested earlier that the mention of "late night basketball playing by kids from the city" was a reference to black cultural differentiation. The black Community Services director who made this statement may not want his own children to be out playing ball at night. What he is expressing is a respect for basketball as an important social activity for some blacks, and a public acknowledgment that he views the failure to provide facilities to carry it out as a failure on the part of Columbia's decision makers to recognize the city's plural population. In a similar vein, the Irish politician who returns to a public religiosity is not simply making an expedient political move, but is also attempting to convey respect for one cultural marker of an ethnic collectivity to which he feels he belongs. Both are in a sense elevating the image of ethnic identity that previously was deemed lower or working class to one of middle-class ethnic pride.

Why then do middle-class whites maintain the cover on the subject of race, and participate in the use of the category "lower income" when often everyone knows the discussion is about blacks? Whites want most of all to protect a comfortable, aesthetically pleasing, middle-class life style, and also to protect their property values. Much of this has to do with the power, to which middle-class whites have become accustomed, to establish within some broad standard the cultural patterns of those with whom they must live and interact in close proximity. One of the reasons whites are fearful of alienating blacks is their recognition of the unfair distribution of resources blacks have been subject to simply because of their color. On the other hand, whites fear blacks who do not assimilate to white middle-class values. Whites speak longingly of a "black community" in Columbia. When they do they are hoping for such an entity to deal with violence between black and white youths in the high school and in public places. What they have in mind is a coalition of middle-class whites and blacks, stronger by virtue of incorporating the legitimacy of the black community, that would define appropriate behavior by some communitywide standard with which they could be comfortable. Although I in no way suggest such a deliberate intent on the part of whites, this would effectively fragment blacks along class lines, and discourage maintenance of black cultural distinctiveness except in the sense of being supplementary to white middle-class culture. Black cultural arts festivals would be one example. Thus, the cover of "lower income" is in some sense a reality for whites. They "know" that blackness implies different cultural standards and they "see" lower income housing in Columbia as mostly, if not all, black. It is these lower income black values that they fear.

The facts of the case in Chapter 6 convey the misleading impression that the major confrontations in this new town reflect power negotiations between lower income residents and the rest of Columbia. This confuses the idiom of these confrontations with the categories of people who are the players in the political drama. Indeed, the idiom of the power struggle is not race, but class. However, when we look more closely at the redefinition of the nature of privilege that is being forged by the actions and reactions in this case, the fact that blacks are unwilling to hand over their power as a source of legitimacy to whites, or even to risk being in the position where there might be public pressure to do so, becomes more understandable. It is also evident that, although it is nearly impossible to find issues and controversies where political collectivism among blacks is overt, the public positions being taken by blacks for lower income residents in general have critical ramifications for the collectivity of blacks.

In short, this is not a cultural struggle over the values of either lower income residents or blacks, but a political struggle over privilege framed in the cultural metaphor of poverty. It is very easy to confuse cultural (values) issues and structural (power) issues when life-style appears to be the bone of contention. These confrontations, and most of those that appear in vignette form throughout the other chapters, represent a power struggle not over *what* is an appropriate life-style, but over *who has the right* to determine how individuals shall conduct their lives. Marshall's success in these confrontations is represented in this paraphrase from an interview he held with the press: We want what we are entitled to as residents of a community that professes the ideology of heterogeneity and equal access, but other than that, I wish the gap between Interfaith and the community would be left alone.

It is well to remember that although Marshall, who is white, never frames his arguments for the rights of lower income residents in terms of race, in the eyes of the community his constituency is black. If the white middle-class community thinks of "the poor" as black while at the same time wording the issues in terms of poverty rather than race, at least one question remains to be asked: Why is there a heavier proscription on categorizing by race than by class? There is an associated question that will begin to let us uncover the complexity in this link between class and race: Why are the poor permitted to be culturally distinct? While much effort is expended to keep lower income residences "up to the standards of Columbia," most white middle-class Columbians agree that this is a hopeless task because "poor people just have different standards." On the other hand, to take a nonderogatory comment in order to strengthen the contrast, it is rare to find a white person today who will go so far as to comment that a black lawyer neighbor dances well simply by virtue of being black. Stereotyping of blacks, either positively or negatively, is no longer permissible. Stereotyping by economic class is still quite acceptable.

It is not considered immoral to explain the behavior of a black person by his blackness. During the period when this was becoming secure as an American norm, however, middle-income blacks temporarily lost all claim to cultural hegemony as they strove to enter the American middle class. Except for gaining more of the material goods of the economic system, they were in some ways more oppressed than before as they tailored their behavior to "fit in." Meanwhile, however, the Horatio Alger myth continued to legitimate the stereotyping of poor people. Those who remain at the bottom of the ladder of socioeconomic prestige, while we are sorry for them and willing to tithe in one way or another to help them, are there because they did not try hard enough. The return they owe us is to act like we do—anything less is unappreciative if not irresponsible.

Most of us agree that we are entitled to find certain behaviors of poor people unacceptable and have developed a phrase (culture of poverty) to explain why these people "have so many children," "buy non-nutritious food with food stamps," and the like. Middle-class blacks in Columbia, however, understand and deeply resent the link in many white people's minds between being poor and being black, and they seem determined, with the support of the Columbia ideology, to let this be known. In the process, whether deliberately or not, they take up the case of cultural oppression of all poor people in Columbia. Moreover, the difference between the treatment of race and class emphasized here is reminiscent of the ideas of Columbia's early planners; namely, middle-class white and black Columbians share a value system that should, if exercised in unison to control potential wayward behavior of lower income people, insure an integrated *and* middle-class community.

SOCIAL CHANGE IN MICROCOSM

Commentators on the Columbia experience have suggested that the ability to develop and maintain a wide mix of residents is the result of early advertising of the social and ethnic mix that was planned for the city. Unlike such other new towns as Irvine, California, where attempts to bring in government-sponsored units after the development of the city was well underway met with considerable opposition from residents, Columbia's success is said to be the result of including a wide range of poeple early in the development process. To put it another way, these analysts suggest that when middle-class immigrants to a community understand that they are in fact choosing to live in a hetergeneous environment, racial and class mixing is more likely to be successful. The evidence for drawing this conclusion seems clear: only Columbia and Reston, Virginia, among the numerous new town developments, advertised a commitment to racial and class integration, and it is only in these two new towns that we find both a significant population mix and acceptance of moves to maintain and further the heterogeneous character of the population. When this accomplishment is understood to be the result of decisions made by middle-class white Americans, it is clear that it was a moral choice to live in such a community and to support policies that would keep a racial and class balance. Thus, the first assumption is that wide knowledge of the mix in the community draws individuals who consider the principle of residential hetero-geneity to be important. Second, since it seems evident that the rather wide perception of an improved quality of life to be attained as a member of the Columbia community is probably at least as important in the decision to move there as a search for heterogeneity, it is assumed that racial and class prejudice is still a factor to be faced, and that a close and continual exposure to different kinds of people will reduce, if not eliminate, the anxiety most middle-class white Americans experience when faced with racial or class mixing of their neighborhoods.

This argument emphasizes psychological variables, and suggests a subtle continuation of the idea, prevalent in the 1960s, that legis-lating morality is difficult. In other words, if by open acknowledgment of the plans to foster an integrated community the people who choose to move there are somewhat more amenable to living in such a situation, then the reality of getting to know blacks or lower income people as neighbors will reinforce and extend these attitudes through the good relationships that will be fostered among different kinds of people. "You can't change people's minds, but you *can* change their hearts" it has been said, and the concern that Columbia residents show about maintaining their balanced community and insuring that the quality of life is equally available to all residents is seen to exemplify this approach.

Although I would suggest that the psychological nature of race and class prejudice is unimportant in understanding situations such as this one, there is another useful way of placing the experience of Columbia in a perspective that addresses the larger issues of open housing by race and by class that face community planners and government public policymakers. Columbia is indeed a small-scale experiment in social change, but it is one where power, not prejudice, is the critical issue at state.

My argument is that the ideology of Columbia and the reality of a socially mixed community dovetail very nicely if the goal is a plural society that does not oppress certain segments. Middle-class Columbians have become prisoners of the ideology that marks their community. Columbia is a good place to live not only because of its clever distribution and use of physical space, its recreational and social amenities, and its innovative school system, but also because, in a time when the rhetoric about equal access and affirmative action is being matched by public action, the largest success of Columbia is its remarkable accomplishment of this end by choice.

While a unique and small-scale social experiment, Columbia affords an opportunity for a close look at processes of social change that are occurring in other, unplanned settings. This opportunity exists because of the presence of categories of residents that are often denied access to such residential environments, and the strength of the ideology that professes an open community marked by equal access to community resources. Together, these provide the raison d'etre for community life. The ethic of participatory democracy that marks the process of decision making both exposes what is happening and makes the process more accessible to new players and new political moves. When outsiders (blacks, lower income families, or other ethnic-like categories) become members of a community, the usual power distribution is open for renegotiation. When the smallest of decisions is argued interminably in public, the opportunity for manipulation of the rhetoric of equality is vastly increased. This does not mean that political collectivism is overt; investigators looking for signs of ethnic coalescing at the political level would find this situation quite barren precisely because of the careful and covert use of the symbols of power as covers in the competition. Nevertheless, just as Leach spoke of the Kachin Hills area, a process of almost imperceptible social change is being encouraged in this community.[11] The raw materials are the mixed population and the ideology; the resource being struggled over is power. The result is an exciting and viable experiment not in integration, as the planners idealistically hoped, but in pluralism.

The mark of a successful politician is skill in manipulating disguised networks of legitimacy. The same is true of informal power relations. The ambiguity inherent in the symbols with which individuals discuss and manipulate their own and others' positions in society allows freedom to maneuver between the egalitarian image of American society and the facts of social stratification on the ground.

These informal groupings tend to be invisible, both to the observer and sometimes to the members themselves. Abner Cohen makes this point in his recent book:

> Through our style of life and social activities, we may develop the interests of a "class" or status group without even realizing

that we are in fact doing so or that we are at all "members" in such a group. There are indeed many groups that are in this sense "invisible" and it is part of the task of the sociology of politics to "discover," identify, and analyze the structure of these groups.[12]

He goes on to point out that the search for these interest groups can be approached from two vantage points: one can either look for evidence of the groups per se by following controversial issues and the persons that appear around them, or one can note symbols that are recurrently used, and attempt to discover groups through tracing the clues provided by the symbols.[13] This research evolved in both modes. Although I was looking for clues to the power relations between different categories of people, I could not presuppose what these categories might be. The goal was to examine the bahavior of visible elites in Columbia, in general professional, well-educated, solidly middle class, and white, as the target group. Continued observation of the obvious political actors in the decision-making process and participation in noncontroversial roles within the system brought to light some areas of interface between this target group, the policymaking elites, and other categories in the community. Once sensitized to some of the controversies that employ the symbol of lower income, I was able to watch for key phrases such as "those people," and "our pools," and to further develop my understanding of the use of these nuances. Moreover, while concentrating on empirical observation of Interfaith residents in an attempt to isolate the discrepancy between Interfaith residents as an actual collectivity of people and the symbol, lower income, as it was used in the manipulation of power, I could monitor at close range the appearance of controversial issues that seemed to surround lower income residents.

Legitimate public issues such as the sliding scale of payment, the extent to which the community wished to support day care, the problems with teen center programming, and the extent to which the architectural review system could control the management of subsidized housing, have become the idioms for negotiation over the nature of privilege. The rhetoric of these cover issues has routinized a change from a polity that operated under the motif, "keep the poor in their place," represented by means tests and Earn-a-Membership programs, to one of "let's make poor people more like us," represented by a concern that lower income residents feel welcome at facilities and that they maintain their property in a manner that reflects middle-class concepts of property values. Chapter 6 set forth the changes that are presently occurring, partly through the institutionalization of an informal power brokerage at the interface between lower income residents and the rest of Columbia. Lower income residents are beginning to remove the cover on the previously unspoken and mandatory reciprocal agreement that has accompanied charitable concessions in the past; namely, that recipients of "unearned" resources such as subsidized housing and lower rates for services based on income level should exchange control over their own life-styles for a share in these resources that belong to the middle class. Leach points out that "another way of regarding phenomena of structural change is to say that we are concerned with shifts in the *focus* of political power within a given system."[14] In Columbia the focus of this kind of structural change is the gradual relinquishing of power by middle-class elites as a result of challenges to their pre-rogatives to establish standards of appropriate conduct according to middle-class values.

This research began as an examination of the symbolic language through which largely white, middle-class Columbians held control of the decision-making process. An equally complex focus emerged early on, and the result is a close look at how a particularly innovative community leader, moving between categories in the role of broker, manipulated this private language for and with lower income residents. This led to changes in the dynamics of the decision-making process, and consequently to changes in the distribution of power. Together these perspectives have uncovered a process of social change that is hardly perceptible to the casual observer because of the hidden language in which it is being negotiated.

CONCLUSION: A PLURAL COMMUNITY

Like any real city of 100,000, Columbia will be economically diverse, polycultural, multi-faith, and interracial.[15]

Perhaps the most enduring myth has developed around the new town. . . . This myth holds that by building new towns, America can solve a number of its urban problems, establish better public services, create new forms of class and racial integration that do no now exist in its cities and suburbs, and implement other innovations.[16]

The first statement above represents the dream of James Rouse and is his conception of the social dimensions of the "Next America" that he hoped to build. The second statement conveys the skepticism of Herbert Gans about the viability of planned, socially heterogeneous communities. Somewhere in between lies a real social phenomenon, Columbia, Maryland, having passed the tenth anniversary of its inception as a racially and socioeconomically mixed new community. Rouse did not envision the social separation between blacks and whites that has occurred, nor did he predict the plethora of interest groups that would emerge along the cultural lines of race, class, religion, age, and marital status. Gans, on the other hand, took a dim view of the possibility that these forms of social fragmentation would have different dimensions than they did in other American communities. Some part of what each of these men predicted can be abstracted from the social dynamic of Columbia, Maryland, in 1976.

This book argues that Columbia is a heterogeneous community that comes closer each day to being a working plural community. In such a community, many of the perceived problems of social fragmentation are best understood as important indicators of the power reorganizations that must of necessity accompany this kind of social experiment. What has happened in Columbia is that the city works as a city, if only in a neophyte stage. Ironically, this success as a city is responsible for the failure of the neighborhood concept, which was based on a suburban model where people were encouraged to form more than superficial ties with their neighbors as a consequence of their mutual isolation from the commercial, cultural, and social centers of the city. In Columbia, residents were supposed to abandon their cars and spend their nonworking hours at neighborhood barbecues, eating food that was purchased from neighborhood "Ma and Pa" stores, after swimming together in their own neighborhood pools. Instead, because of the diversity that does exist and because some attempt has been made to duplicate a real city with a range of religious and cultural facilities, friends can be drawn from one's religious or interest group associations. Moreover, these friendships can be easily pursued because of the manageable size of the city. In other words, the failure of the neighborhood concept is one important indicator that Columbia works as a heterogeneous community.

Another such indication is that while black and white adults in Columbia live happily next door to one another, work, shop, swim, and parent together, they choose to spend their most relaxed, pleasure-oriented times with other blacks or other whites, while hesitating to substantiate this verbally. At the same time, issues in the public arena that touch on black concerns, while often argued in the idiom of class rather than race, are quietly but persistently approached as if there were indeed an identifiable black polity. Moreover, race is not the only indicator that the richness of cultural roots is fostered in this mixed community. One organization for singles (itself a marker of age and marital status as important variants of Columbia's mixed population) has evolved into several separate organizations, including a black and a Jewish group.

The planners of Columbia worked with a dichotomy in their heads, one that is suggested by the two quotations at the beginning of this section. Rouse and his team of innovative planners, committed as they were to a mixed and balanced community, saw assimilation as the only viable alternative to social fragmentation and hostility. The residents of Columbia, albeit unwittingly, have taken the raw materials provided by the ideology of integration and molded the dimensions of the community into a stable and working pluralism that respects and builds on the variations in its population. One well-known example of this is the Interfaith Center, a large modern structure planned and built to house numerous different religious groups. These different groups indeed occupy the center today, but they do not form one comfortable interdenominational effort; rather, each competes, at times rather fiercely, for an equitable share of the expenses and the resources available to them as tenants of one physical structure.

Pluralism in Columbia lies on a continuum between the polar opposites of fragmentation and assimilation, between the extreme where breakdowns in communication bring about fences or race riots, and its opposite where the weaker sectors of the population, either by coercion or the promise of rewards from the more powerful sector, assume the mainline values of the community. Pluralism is marked by overt and covert negotiation between categories of persons. Thus, to be a pluralistic community, "gaps are a prerequisite;[17]" the differences that exist between people cannot be institutinalized away by assimilation, nor can minorities be subordinated to a powerless status. Rather, the presence of different categories of people is the bony structure of the informal political organization of the community.

The lack of fit between the ideology of Columbia that emphasizes equality and equal access in the context of racial and socioeconomic hetergeneity, and the actual system of privilege that exists
is mediated by a system of symbols, a private language that objectifies
the discrepancy between the ideal and the real with terms that carry
enough ambiguity to allow for changes in the focus of power. These
changes can be seen in challenges to the power of the middle class as
their right to determine appropriate values for all categories of
individuals is threatened. The ambiguity inherent in symbols that
seem to reflect the confrontation as one of class (for example, property
values, lower income, multifamily) is being cleverly and covertly
exploited by blacks with the acquiescence of lower income whites.
These negotiations, while employing only the idiom of class, represent
indirect power struggles between blacks and whites as well as poor
and nonpoor. It is important that we understand these power struggles
as positive signs of social change if the moves to end racial and socioeconomic discrimination and oppression in our society are to continue.

NOTES

1   *New York Times*, January 13, 1980
2   Huber 1974:339
3   Hannerz 1969
4   Liebow 1967
5   Barth 1966
6   Liebow 1967:65
7   Rainwater 1970
8   Schaffer 1970
9   Hartman 1969
10   Leach 1954:10
11   Leach 1954
12   Cohen 1974:66
13   Cohen 1974:130
14   Leach 1954:9
15   Rouse 1967:5
16   Gans 1973:137
17   Paine 1974:27

BIBLIOGRAPHY

Advisory Committee to the Department of Housing and Urban Development. 1972. *Freedom of Choice in Housing: Opportunities and Constraints.* Washington, D.C.: National Academy of Sciences, National Academy of Engineering.

Bailey, F. G. 1969. *Stratagems and Spoils: A Social Anthropology of Politics.* Oxford: Blackwell.

Barth, Fredrik. 1966. "Models of Social Organization," Royal Anthropological Institute Occasional Paper No. 23. London: Royal Anthropological Institute.

Bott, Elizabeth. 1971. *Family and Social Network: Roles, Norms, and External Relationships in Ordinary Urban Families.* 2d ed. London: Tavistock.

Burby, Raymond J. III, and Shirley F. Weiss. 1976. *New Communities U.S.A.* Lexington, Mass.: D.C. Heath.

Campbell, Angus. 1971. *White Attitudes toward Black People.* Ann Arbor: University of Michigan.

Cohen, Abner. 1969. "Political Anthropology: The Analysis of the Symbolism of Power Relations." *Man* 4 (2):215-35.

——. 1974. *Two-Dimensional Man: An Essay on the Anthropology of Power and Symbolism in Complex Society.* London: Routledge and Kegan Paul.

——. 1979. "Political Symbolism." In *Annual Review of Anthropology* 8:87-113.

Columbia Association. 1972a. "Citizen Participation in the Roles Study."

——. 1972b. "Columbia Task Force Report: Summary and Recommendations."

——. 1973. "Neighborhood Evaluation Survey."

———. 1974a. "Goals, Objectives, and Policies of the Columbia Association."

———. 1974b. "The Briefing Book: Background Materials on the Columbia Association and on the Village Associations of Columbia."

———. 1974c. Columbia Demographic Analysis Series. Office of Planning and Evaluation.

Dumont, Louis. 1970. *Homo Hierarchicus: The Case System and Its Implications*. London: Weidenfeld and Nicholson.

Fallers, Lloyd A. 1974. *The Social Anthropology of a Nation-State*. Chicago: Aldine.

Fortes, Meyer. 1970. *Time and Social Structure and Other Essays*. New York: Humanities.

Gans, Herbert. 1973. "The Possibility of Class and Racial Integration in American New Towns: A Policy-Oriented Analysis." In *New Towns: Why and For Whom?*, ed. Harvey S. Perloff and Neil C. Sandberg. New York: Praeger.

Goffman, Erving. 1959. *The Presentation of Self in Everyday Life*. Garden City, N.Y.: Doubleday Anchor.

———. 1961. *Asylums: Essays on the Social Situation of Mental Patients and Other Inmates*. Garden City, N.Y.: Doubleday Anchor.

Hannerz, Ulf. 1969. *Soulside: Inquiries into Ghetto Culture and Community*. New York: Columbia University.

Hartman, Chester. 1969. "The Politics of Housing." In *Political Power and the Urban Crisis*, ed. Alan Shank. Boston: Holbrook Press.

Hollander, Sydney and Associates. 1972. *Problems and Prospects in Columbia: An Attitude Survey*. Columbia: The Columbia Association.

Huber, Joan. 1974. "Programs against Poverty: Epilogue." In *The Sociology of American Poverty*, ed. Joan Huber and Peter Chalfant. Cambridge: Schenkman.

Leach, E. R. 1954. *Political Systems of Highland Burma: A Study of Kachin Social Structure*. Boston: Beacon Press.

Liebow, Elliot. 1967. *Tally's Corner: A Study of Negro Streetcorner Men*. Boston: Little, Brown.

Moore, Sally. 1972. "Legal Liability and Evolutionary Interpretation: Some Aspects of Strict Liability, Self-Help, and Collective Responsibility." In

The Allocation of Responsibility, ed. Max Gluckman. Manchester: University of Manchester.

Paine, Robert. 1974. "Second Thoughts on Barth's Models." Royal Anthropological Institute Occasional Paper No. 32. London: Royal Anthropological Institute.

Rainwater, Lee. 1970. *Behind Ghetto Walls.* Chicago: Aldine.

Rossi, Peter H. 1968. "Power and Community Structure." In *Community Structure and Decision-Making: Comparative Analyses,* ed. Terry N. Clark. San Francisco: Chandler.

Rouse, James W. 1967. "Cities That Work for Man — Victory Ahead." An address delivered at the Lions International/University of Puerto Rico Symposium on "The City of the Future."

Schaffer, Frank. 1970. *The New Town Story.* London: MacGibbon and Kee.

Turner, V. W. 1957. *Schism and Continuity in an African Society: A Study of Ndembu Village Life.* Manchester: University of Manchester.

Vincent, Joan. 1978. Political Anthropology: Manipulative Strategies." In *Annual Review of Anthropology* 1:175-94.

Warner, W. Lloyd, and Paul S. Lunt. 1941. *The Social Life of a Modern Community.* New Haven: Yale University Press.

INDEX

ABOUT THE AUTHOR

LYNNE BURKHART earned a Ph. D. in Social Relations from the Johns Hopkins University in 1975. In order to carry out the in-depth research on which this book is based, she and her family moved to Columbia, Maryland, a city where subsidized and middle-income residents shared backyards. Dr. Burkhart later worked as urban policy advisor to former Secretary of Transportation, Brock Adams. Dr. Burkhart is now working on a book about the relationship between transportation investments and urban dislocation and gentrification.